Learning Ansible

Embrace productivity and challenge IT complexity with the best automation engine

AF675183

Wayne Taylor

GitforGits™
ASIAN PUBLISHING HOUSE

Copyright © 2023 by GitforGits

All rights reserved. This book is protected under copyright laws and no part of it may be reproduced or transmitted in any form or by any means, electronic or mechanical, including photocopying, recording, or by any information storage and retrieval system, without the prior written permission of the publisher. Any unauthorized reproduction, distribution, or transmission of this work may result in civil and criminal penalties and will be dealt with in the respective jurisdiction at anywhere in India, in accordance with the applicable copyright laws.

Published by: GitforGits
Publisher: Sonal Dhandre
www.gitforgits.com
support@gitforgits.com

Printed in India

First Printing: October 2023

ISBN: 9788119177592

Cover Design by: Kitten Publishing

For permission to use material from this book, please contact GitforGits at support@gitforgits.com.

Prologue

Due to Ansible's meteoric rise to prominence in the fields of cloud orchestration, DevOps, and IT automation, a thorough familiarity with its many features and functions is now required. "Learning Ansible" is designed to be a definitive resource for anyone looking to enhance their abilities in this dynamic and ever-changing industry, whether they are complete beginners or seasoned pros. This book is designed to be a thorough introduction to the world of Ansible, with real-world examples, illustrations, and hands-on activities supporting the content at every step.

Every chapter builds upon the previous one, revealing the intricate web of tasks that Ansible can complete. The book starts with an introduction to Ansible's architecture and fundamental principles and then proceeds to cover a wide range of subjects. The first few chapters lay out the groundwork for automation by introducing key concepts and explaining their roles, tasks, modules, and templates. To maintain a well-rounded education, the theoretical underpinnings are always supplemented with practical examples.

The book's middle section dives into more specialized domains, covering topics like workstation automation, cron jobs, user management, and system administration. The following chapters provide an in-depth look at network automation, covering topics such as automating configuration, software upgrades, and common network problem troubleshooting. The goal of this in-depth examination of these topics is to help readers become future-ready IT professionals by providing them with the tools they need to deal with real-world situations.

This book focuses heavily on integration, showing how Ansible works with different platforms and tools. The reader is led step-by-step through the process, removing the mystery from connecting to various cloud providers like AWS and Azure, as well as popular tools like Jenkins, Docker, and Kubernetes. The inclusion of various integrations guarantees a broader view, which in turn helps to cultivate an appreciation for Ansible's ability to accomplish seamless orchestration.

With its emphasis on pedagogical consistency, "Learning Ansible" stands out. The book maintains cohesion in its teaching by repeatedly using a typical web server as an example. This recurring theme helps to solidify the ideas, making it easier for you to understand how everything fits together. Chapters devoted to common mistakes, performance bottlenecks, security vulnerabilities, and how to fix them show that debugging and security were not neglected. By the end of these chapters, you should be able to code with more precision and self-assurance, ready to face any problems that crop up in a production setting.

In the end, the book covers all the topics and approaches with a full-stack application setup using Ansible. This final product demonstrates Ansible's capabilities in all their glory, inspiring readers to delve deeper and find solutions that fit their specific needs. More than just a technical knowledge book, "Learning Ansible" takes you on a journey into a field that is changing the face of IT and how it is implemented. This book is a must-have for anyone aspiring to master Ansible and IT automation. It covers all the bases, explains everything clearly, and takes a practical approach. After finishing this book, readers will have gained more than just knowledge of Ansible. They will have absorbed a philosophy of automation that will undoubtedly influence their career path.

Content

Preface

To help aspiring IT professionals succeed in the automation field, "Learning Ansible" provides an in-depth primer that covers all the essential skills. The book is an excellent resource that will help you become an expert IT automation specialist and Ansible Developer.

Starting with an introduction to Ansible, the journey will show how crucial it is in today's IT settings. The first few chapters cover the essentials, diving into topics like configuration management, automation, integration, and orchestration. The authors make sure that you can confidently troubleshoot issues by thoroughly examining network, performance, and security errors and providing advanced debugging techniques. Practical uses of Ansible in system administration, user and group management, and managing common and complex errors are explored throughout the book. Setup of network devices, software upgrade automation, and fixing recurring network problems are all covered in detail, along with example programs.

Next, we'll take a closer look at DevOps, with a focus on how Ansible has impacted CI/CD pipelines. The book teaches you how to integrate Ansible with popular tools and cloud providers like AWS and Azure through hands-on demonstrations. These tools include Jenkins, Docker, Kubernetes, and more.

Additionally, integration is extended to databases such as MySQL and MongoDB, as well as monitoring tools such as Nagios and Prometheus. By incorporating practical exercises throughout, the book guarantees that you will grasp the concepts and be able to put them to use in actual situations.

In this book you will learn how to:

- A thorough introduction to Ansible, laying the groundwork for mastering IT automation techniques.
- In-depth examination of system administration, with emphasis on improving user and group management skills.
- Detailed instructions for debugging in Ansible, enhancing problem-solving and troubleshooting abilities.
- Practical demonstrations of network device configuration, aimed at improving network management skills.
- Hands-on Ansible integration with Jenkins, Docker, and Kubernetes, enhancing CI/CD capabilities.
- Integration with cloud providers such as AWS and Azure to strengthen cloud management skills.

- Techniques for automating workstation setup and software upgrades, with the goal of increasing automation efficiency.
- Integration with monitoring and logging tools, promoting best practices in system monitoring.
- Using Ansible to build a full-stack application setup and gain end-to-end automation expertise.
- Consistent application of web server sample program, which makes learning practical and relatable.

GitforGits

Prerequisites

"Learning Ansible" serves as a definitive resource for those aiming to automate, simplify, and accelerate their IT processes. Its detailed insights and hands-on practices offer a pathway to not only becoming proficient in Ansible but also mastering the broader spectrum of IT Automation. Whether you are a beginner eager to get started or a seasoned professional looking to enhance your skills, this book is a valuable addition to your toolkit, guiding you towards efficiency, scalability, and innovation in your IT endeavors."

Codes Usage

Are you in need of some helpful code examples to assist you in your programming and documentation? Look no further! Our book offers a wealth of supplemental material, including code examples and exercises.

Not only is this book here to aid you in getting your job done, but you have our permission to use the example code in your programs and documentation. However, please note that if you are reproducing a significant portion of the code, we do require you to contact us for permission.

But don't worry, using several chunks of code from this book in your program or answering a question by citing our book and quoting example code does not require permission. But if you do choose to give credit, an attribution typically includes the title, author, publisher, and ISBN. For example, "Learning Ansible by Wayne Taylor".

If you are unsure whether your intended use of the code examples falls under fair use or the permissions outlined above, please do not hesitate to reach out to us at support@gitforgits.com.

We are happy to assist and clarify any concerns.

Acknowledgement

I owe a tremendous debt of gratitude to GitforGits, for their unflagging enthusiasm and wise counsel throughout the entire process of writing this book. Their knowledge and careful editing helped make sure the piece was useful for people of all reading levels and comprehension skills. In addition, I'd like to thank everyone involved in the publishing process for their efforts in making this book a reality. Their efforts, from copyediting to advertising, made the project what it is today.

Finally, I'd like to express my gratitude to everyone who has shown me unconditional love and encouragement throughout my life. Their support was crucial to the completion of this book. I appreciate your help with this endeavour and your continued interest in my career.

CHAPTER 1: INTRODUCTION TO ANSIBLE

Automation Landscape Overview

In the ever-changing landscape of technology, the rise of DevOps and the rise of software automation have marked a significant revolution. ANSIBLE automation has been at the forefront of this revolution. Together, they signify a shift towards processes that are more agile, efficient, and streamlined, all of which are essential in the modern era. The current climate of the information technology industry is characterized by an unrelenting drive towards innovation, speed, and adaptability. Long gone are the days when companies could afford protracted development cycles or tolerate siloed operations between development and operations teams. Today's businesses simply cannot afford to operate in such a manner. Businesses of today need to be nimble and efficient in order to keep up with the ever-shifting demands of their customers, the ever-advancing technological landscape, and the ever-changing market.

Need for Automation

The need for automation has emerged as a central component in the process of responding to these challenges. By automating tasks that are mundane, error-prone, and repetitive, businesses are able to reallocate their employees' attention to activities that add more value to the company, such as innovation, problem solving, and other creative endeavours. Not only does automation lessen the likelihood of mistakes made by humans, but it also quickens the pace of process, which enables businesses to provide their goods and services more quickly. It has made its way into every facet of the software development lifecycle, from coding and testing to deployment and monitoring of the software. Through the use of automation, there has been a significant improvement in the capacity to manage and exercise control over configurations in a variety of environments. IT professionals now have the ability to codify configurations using tools such as Ansible, which ensures consistency, repeatability, and scalability across a variety of systems and platforms. The impact of automation is perhaps most obvious in the field of continuous integration and continuous delivery (CI/CD), where it has made it possible to integrate and deploy code changes without any interruptions. This continuous flow ensures that new features, bug fixes, and updates can be integrated, tested, and deployed quickly, which in turn reduces the amount of time it takes to go from development to production.

DevOps Revolution

DevOps is both a cultural and methodological shift that has fundamentally transformed the way in which development and operations teams collaborate with one another. This union is a synergy that fosters communication, collaboration, integration, and automation; it is more than just a simple combination of development and operations. The DevOps methodology encourages the use of a shared responsibility model, which helps to eliminate conventional roadblocks and boosts team collaboration. This collaboration helps to foster a more cohesive approach to the delivery of software, in which each stage is interconnected and aligned with the goals of the organization. DevOps is a process that improves efficiency and cuts down on the amount of time it takes to bring a product to market. It does this by employing automation tools, sharing best practices, and working together. It provides a framework that ensures quality, security, and performance are fundamental components throughout the entire lifecycle of the product. The current climate of software automation and the revolution brought about by DevOps represent a sea change in the manner in which technology is approached, developed, and delivered. It places an emphasis on things like responsiveness, agility, quality, and collaboration. Tools that enable automation, such as Ansible, play a crucial part in enabling organisations to adapt to this new era by providing the means to manage complex systems in an effective and confident manner. This is one of the most important roles that these tools play. In the chapters that follow, we will delve deeper into the particulars of Ansible, gaining an understanding of how it fits into this landscape, as well as how IT professionals can harness its power to meet the demands of contemporary software development and operations.

Why Ansible?

As the landscape of software development evolved, with an increasing need for agility, speed, and consistency, the search for solutions to automate various processes became crucial. The challenge was to find tools that were simple yet powerful, scalable yet flexible, and capable of unifying diverse aspects of development, deployment, and operations. Ansible emerged as a solution that met these needs, fitting seamlessly into both software automation and the DevOps culture.

Brief Overview

Ansible is an open-source automation tool that allows for configuration management, application deployment, task automation, and even multi-tier orchestration. Built on simplicity and ease of use, Ansible uses YAML, a human-readable language, to define automation jobs, making it accessible for developers, sysadmins, and IT professionals. Ansible works by connecting to machines over SSH and executing tasks in order, making it fast and reliable. It also has no agents or additional software to install on client machines. Ansible can be used for a wide variety of automation tasks like provisioning infrastructure, deploying applications, automating day-to-day maintenance, and more. It has a large library of modules that make all kinds of tasks quick and easy. Ansible is agentless, using OpenSSH and WinRM for remote execution. Overall, Ansible is a powerful yet simple way to automate processes and configure systems across an organization.

Evolution of Software Automation

Modern systems are incredibly complex, often comprising various technologies, platforms, and environments. Managing these systems manually was becoming increasingly error-prone, time-consuming, and challenging as complexity grew. The market was saturated with specialized tools that handled individual aspects of development and operations, but there was no unified platform. Organizations needed to stitch together disjointed solutions to automate processes. This fractured landscape motivated the creation of a new breed of tooling. Ansible emerged as a platform that could bring together these diverse needs into one cohesive, easy-to-use automation framework. Built for simplicity and reliability, Ansible relies on commonly available technologies like SSH and

YAML to orchestrate systems at scale. Ansible's agentless architecture and vast library of modules gave it the flexibility and power to automate everything from network devices to cloud infrastructure. By providing a unified automation platform, Ansible enabled organizations to efficiently manage complex, multi-faceted IT environments with ease.

Ansible as a Solution

Simplifying Complexity

Ansible's agentless architecture and simple YAML-based language made it accessible and easy to implement, even for those without specialized skills. By abstracting complex processes into declarative playbooks, Ansible allowed users to manage intricate systems and workflows without needing to be experts. Its emphasis on simplicity opened automation to a wider audience beyond just developers and seasoned sysadmins. Ansible used SSH to connect to machines and execute tasks, removing the need for installing agents. Playbooks provided a human-readable format for users to define automation jobs in simple language. The low learning curve enabled rapid onboarding and quick wins for automating manual, repetitive administration tasks. Ansible gave organizations the power to simplify complexity.

Flexibility and Extensibility

Ansible's modular design, with thousands of available modules, made it adaptable to a diverse array of use cases within an enterprise. Modules encapsulated specific system tasks and abstracted away implementation details. Playbooks combined modules to deliver complete automation flows, from executing simple administration tasks to orchestrating complex multi-tier applications. Ansible could automate the provisioning and configuration of infrastructure, deploy application code, handle continuous delivery pipelines, and manage long-running services. Its flexibility allowed it to adapt to an organization's specific environment and needs through custom modules. Ansible enabled teams to start small with simple task automation and scale up to advanced orchestration of their entire IT infrastructure.

Enhancing Collaboration

By providing a unified automation platform, Ansible facilitated collaboration between development and operations teams. It enabled a shared understanding of infrastructure-as-code concepts, code deployment, and configuration management. Ansible's simple declarative approach meant developers could define infrastructure requirements and system configurations in ansible playbooks. Meanwhile, sysadmins gained insight into application architecture and deployment processes by implementing the automation. Ansible complemented the DevOps culture well, helping to break down barriers between traditionally siloed roles. Developers gained autonomy to deploy their applications using Ansible automation. Shared ownership of automation code enhanced communication between teams. Ansible delivered a common language that enabled Dev and Ops to collaborate more closely.

Driving the DevOps Transition

Ansible accelerated the DevOps transformation by enabling practices like continuous integration/continuous delivery and infrastructure-as-code. Its agentless nature provided speed and reliability to replace brittle script-based approaches. Ansible allowed version controlling all automation code alongside application code, ensuring consistency between environments. By treating infrastructure as code, Ansible enabled teams to apply software development disciplines like versioning, testing, and peer reviews to operations tasks. Ansible integrated with CI/CD pipelines to enable repeatable deployments and updates. Automating deployment processes enabled teams to ship changes rapidly and frequently. Ansible helped drive the inflection point where automation shifted from an aspiration to the new standard. It enabled organizations to remove roadblocks and silos holding back the DevOps transition.

Empowering Innovation

By providing robust automation capabilities out-of-the-box, Ansible empowered teams to focus their efforts on innovation rather than infrastructure maintenance. Organizations could allocate more time for developing value-adding capabilities with reduced engineering overhead spent on mundane upkeep. Ansible unlocked developer productivity by enabling self-service provisioning of test environments without waiting on operations. Its composable modules enabled teams to build higher-level abstractions tailored to their needs. Ansible reduced organizational friction through reliable, scalable automation that just worked. This freed up resources to work on innovation and new capabilities that delivered true business value.

DevOps Journey with Ansible

Configuration Management

Ansible excelled at configuration management, ensuring consistency across systems by enforcing desired state. Ansible playbooks defined and managed system configurations in a simple, declarative language. This allowed development, testing, and production environments to remain uniform, reducing the "works on my machine" problem that plagued software teams. Ansible enabled push-button deployment of configurations to rapidly setup systems. Its idempotent nature meant playbooks could be run repeatedly while only applying changes needed to achieve specified state. Ansible gave teams the ability to standardize and lock down configurations across the stack. This enhanced collaboration since issues could be replicated and debugged reliably. Ansible brought order and repeatability to managing system configurations.

Continuous Integration and Deployment

Ansible's simple yet powerful automation capabilities made it an integral part of streamlining the CI/CD pipeline. Ansible playbooks could automate the entire workflow from integrating code changes to testing and ultimately deployment. For testing phases, Ansible provided quick provisioning and configuration of temporary environments. Tests could be executed against real instances that matched production. Ansible enabled seamless handoff of built artifacts to deployment roles. For releases, Ansible's push-based deployments provided speed and reliability compared to pull-based approaches. Integrating Ansible as the automation backbone resulted in smooth, automated DevOps pipelines. It removed friction and human overhead, accelerating development cycles.

Infrastructure as Code (IaC)

Ansible enabled infrastructure to be provisioned, managed, and decommissioned by version-controlled definition files. System configurations and infrastructure blueprints could be treated as code. This infrastructure-as-code approach allowed teams to extend software engineering best practices like versioning, testing, and reviews to operations tasks. Ansible playbooks gave teams ability to rebuild and replicate infrastructure on-demand. IaC enabled consistency, transparency, and enabled auto-scaling capabilities essential for cloud-based infrastructure. By bridging the gap between applications and operations, Ansible allowed organizations to unify their tooling. Just as Ansible managed applications, it could also build, configure, and update the underlying infrastructure.

Security and Compliance

Ansible provided modules to automate security policy enforcement and hardening across the environment. Playbooks could implement role-based access controls, firewall policies, encrypted communications, and regularly apply OS security patches. Ansible automation gave visibility into drift and non-compliance. Playbooks codified complex compliance policies like PCI or HIPAA as code. Ansible enabled continuous security monitoring and remediation as part of the software delivery lifecycle. It facilitated a shift left on security - addressing vulnerabilities earlier in development processes. Ansible aligned with DevSecOps practices focusing on baking security into delivery pipelines versus bolting it on afterwards. Its automation capabilities helped enforce security standards at enterprise scale.

Centralized Orchestration

Ansible Tower provided a web-based console and REST API for controlling, sharing, and managing Ansible automation. Ansible Tower enabled centralized orchestration rather than isolated automation. In multi-team environments, Ansible Tower helped coordinate Ansible jobs across business units while providing RBAC controls. Tower provided visibility into job performance, alerting, scheduled execution, and graphical inventory management. As organizations scaled automation complexity, Ansible Tower added structure and governance without taking away Ansible's flexibility.

Fostering Collaboration

By providing a common automation platform, Ansible enabled improved collaboration between teams involved in the application lifecycle. Developers used Ansible to provision infrastructure and deploy their applications. Operations used Ansible to configure production systems and monitor for issues. Sharing Ansible code and workflows fostered improved empathy and insight between roles traditionally siloed. Ansible helped foster a culture that valued collaboration powered by alignment through shared tooling and practices.

The subsequent chapters will delve deeper into Ansible's features, capabilities, and real-world applications, demonstrating why it has become a tool of choice for so many in the field of software automation and DevOps.

Core Capabilities of Ansible

In this subsequent section, we will continue our understanding of Ansible as a potent automation tool by delving into each of its primary capabilities. Because of its extensive feature set, Ansible is well-suited for a diverse array of applications, ranging from straightforward configuration management to in-depth orchestration.

Following is an in-depth look at Ansible capabilities:

Configuration Management

- Definition: Ensures that systems are configured to a specific state, consistent across environments.
- Use: Managing packages, users, services, files, etc.
- Benefit: Reduces human error, ensures consistency, and streamlines system setup.

Task Automation

- Definition: Automates repetitive tasks across multiple machines.
- Use: Regular system updates, batch processing, scheduled jobs.
- Benefit: Saves time, reduces the chance of manual mistakes, allows for scheduling.

Application Deployment

- Definition: Automates the process of deploying applications across environments.
- Use: Rolling updates, zero-downtime deployments, scaling applications.
- Benefit: Speeds up deployment, ensures consistency, and reduces the risk of deployment failures.

Provisioning

- Definition: Automates the process of setting up new servers and infrastructure components.

- Use: Cloud provisioning, virtual machine setup, container orchestration.
- Benefit: Reduces provisioning time, ensures standardization, and allows for scalability.

Orchestration

- Definition: Coordinates and manages the execution of complex, multi-tier application deployments.
- Use: Coordinating start-up and shutdown sequences, managing dependencies.
- Benefit: Simplifies complex deployments, ensures proper sequence execution, enhances maintainability.

Continuous Integration and Continuous Deployment (CI/CD)

- Definition: Integrates automation into the development pipeline for continuous testing, integration, and deployment.
- Use: Automating build processes, testing, staging, and production deployment.
- Benefit: Faster development cycles, higher quality code, more frequent and reliable releases.

Security and Compliance

- Definition: Manages security policies and ensures that systems adhere to compliance standards.
- Use: Enforcing security policies, automating compliance checks.
- Benefit: Streamlines security management, ensures adherence to standards, enhances security posture.

Infrastructure as Code (IaC)

- Definition: Treats infrastructure setup and configuration as code, which can be versioned and maintained.
- Use: Storing infrastructure configurations in version control, enabling repeatability.
- Benefit: Enhances collaboration, enables versioning, ensures consistency across environments.

Ansible's core functionalities offer a comprehensive toolset that addresses various automation needs in modern IT environments. From simplifying repetitive tasks to orchestrating complex, multi-tier deployments, Ansible's features are designed to increase efficiency, consistency, and reliability. Its accessible design, coupled with its powerful capabilities, positions Ansible as a vital tool for professionals engaged in software automation and DevOps practices.

As we proceed through the following chapters, we'll delve into each of these functionalities in detail, exploring practical applications, best practices, and real-world examples to equip you with a deep understanding of Ansible's full potential.

Ansible's Architecture

Understanding Ansible's architecture is essential for grasping how it functions, enabling users to utilize its full potential effectively. Ansible's architecture is designed for simplicity and ease of use. It operates on an agentless model, meaning that there is no need to install additional software on the target machines.

The architecture comprises several key components, each playing a crucial role in Ansible's operations as below:

Control Node

The control node is essentially the orchestrator, a centralized system where Ansible is installed, and from where all tasks are coordinated. When you initiate a task in Ansible, the control node translates this task into a module that gets dispatched to the target system. While the installation process for Ansible on this control node is relatively straightforward, this machine must have Python installed to interact with the managed nodes. The importance of the control node can't be overstated; it's the interface through which administrators manage configurations, deployments, and orchestrations. Whether it's a developer's machine or a centralized server, understanding the control node's setup and capabilities is vital for effective Ansible operation.

Target Nodes

Ansible's agentless architecture simplifies the entire setup process. Target nodes, also known as managed nodes, are those that Ansible manages. You don't need to install any additional software on these nodes, which significantly reduces setup time and minimizes the potential for conflicts or vulnerabilities that agents might introduce. You only need to ensure that the control node can SSH into the target nodes. The list of target nodes is defined in the inventory file, another cornerstone of Ansible's architecture.

Inventory

The inventory is a structured document that lists all the hosts and groups of hosts that Ansible manages. You can organize this document in several ways, categorizing hosts based on their function, location, or some other criteria. Ansible allows for nested groups, enabling a hierarchical structure for more complex environments. The inventory system is versatile, supporting both static and dynamic lists. While static inventories are straightforward text files, dynamic inventories are usually scripts that pull data from external sources like cloud providers or LDAP systems. The depth and flexibility of Ansible's inventory system allow for intricate setups suitable for multi-tier applications and microservices architectures.

Modules

Ansible comes with a plethora of built-in modules that serve specific purposes: there are modules for networking, modules for cloud services, modules for databases, and so on. These modules are like the Swiss Army knives of Ansible; they're purpose-built for specific tasks and are designed to be idempotent, meaning they won't make changes if they detect that the system is already in the desired state. This idempotency is an essential feature that prevents unintended changes and ensures reliability. Advanced users can also create custom modules using Python, allowing for unlimited extensibility. Understanding the function and capabilities of various modules is like mastering the tools in a toolbox, each with its own particular utility and function.

Playbooks

Playbooks are the heart of Ansible's automation capability. They're YAML-formatted text files where you define what Ansible should do. A playbook can contain one or many plays, and each play can contain one or many tasks. The tasks call Ansible's modules to perform some action. You can define variables, loops, and conditionals in playbooks, making them incredibly versatile. You can orchestrate multi-tier rollouts, create complex workflows, and even handle errors gracefully. A single playbook can start with provisioning a virtual machine, move to installing software packages, update firewall rules, and conclude by sending a report email.

Roles

Roles are another advanced feature that brings reusability and organization to playbooks. Roles allow you to bundle automation content and make it reusable, enabling you to break complex setups into smaller, reusable components. Roles are essentially playbooks broken down into a known file structure, which allows for easier sharing and reusing. This is a vital feature for large projects where different teams might work on various aspects of the infrastructure. Role-based access control (RBAC) is often applied at this stage to ensure only authorized personnel can execute specific roles, adding another layer of security.

Plugins

Plugins are small pieces of code that extend Ansible's core functionality. They are a way to execute specific types of tasks in a more streamlined manner than would be possible by just using modules and playbooks. Ansible comes pre-packaged with a variety of plugins, but you can also write your own. These can be written in any programming language that can return JSON, although Python is most commonly used. Examples of plugins include inventory plugins, which can pull in inventory information from various sources, and filter plugins, which can manipulate data within templates.

Configuration File

Ansible uses a configuration file (ansible.cfg) to manage settings like default inventory, privilege escalation, and syntax behaviors. While Ansible does have default settings, you can override them either in this global file or within individual project directories. Understanding how to manipulate this file can greatly enhance Ansible's effectiveness in specialized environments. For instance, you can customize the SSH settings, specify a different inventory file, or even add a notification callback URL where Ansible can send event data.

Vault

The Ansible Vault is a secure place where you can store sensitive data. Any text file can be encrypted using Ansible Vault, be it a variable file, a playbook, or even raw data. Given that playbooks often contain sensitive information like passwords or API keys, the ability to keep this information secure within the same repository as your code is invaluable. The Vault can be secured using a password, and there are multiple ways to provide this password during playbook execution, including plaintext files, prompts, or even a third-party service.

Facts

When Ansible runs, it gathers facts about the target system: details about the hardware, the operating system, IP addresses, available disk spaces, and more. This information is stored in variables that you can use in playbooks and templates. The fact-gathering process is usually the first task in the playbook execution unless disabled. These facts allow you to tailor your automation tasks based on the state of the target system.

Templates

Templates are text files that can contain variables. Ansible uses the Jinja2 templating engine for transforming data inside a template. This allows you to dynamically generate host files or any other text files based on variables. Templates come in handy when you have to deal with configurations that differ only slightly from one server to another. Instead of maintaining multiple nearly-identical files, you maintain one template.

Filters

Filters are another feature borrowed from the Jinja2 templating engine. These are used within template expressions and playbooks to transform and manipulate data. Filters can change the case of text, perform mathematical calculations, manipulate lists, and even create JSON data structures.

Conditionals and Loops

Conditionals and loops bring logic into playbooks. Conditionals are implemented using the when keyword and can skip tasks based on the evaluation of an expression. Loops are implemented using the loop keyword and can run tasks multiple times with different data.

Networking and APIs

Although Ansible began primarily as a tool for managing servers, its capabilities have expanded to manage network devices, storage arrays, and more. Through modules and plugins that interact with APIs, Ansible can manage virtually anything that can be programmatically controlled. This ability has turned Ansible into a universal language of automation, not just for systems administrators but also for network engineers and other IT professionals.

Parallelism and Asynchrony

One of the powerful features of Ansible is its ability to execute multiple tasks in parallel, cutting down on task execution time. Ansible also supports asynchronous task execution, allowing you to kick off a task and move on to the next one without waiting for it to finish.

Ad-hoc Commands

Ansible allows you to perform quick tasks that don't necessarily need a playbook. These are called Ad-Hoc commands and are great for tasks that you might need to execute quickly to fix something or do a one-time operation.

By fully understanding Ansible's architecture and its constituent components, you are better equipped to utilize its power to the fullest. From understanding the basic elements like the control node and inventory to grasping more advanced features like roles, vaults, and custom modules, the architecture provides a solid foundation upon which you can build an automated, efficient, and secure IT infrastructure.

Install Ansible on Linux

Following are the step-by-step instructions for identifying the latest version of Ansible and then installing it:

Finding latest Ansible Version

- Visit Ansible's Official Website: Go to Ansible's website and look for the latest release information.
- Use Package Manager (Optional): On some distributions, you can query the latest version using package managers like apt or yum.

Preparing System

Before you install Ansible, make sure your system is updated.

- On Debian-based systems (like Ubuntu), run:

```
sudo apt-get update
sudo apt-get upgrade
```

- On RedHat-based systems (like CentOS), run:

```
sudo yum update
```

Installing Ansible

The installation process can vary slightly depending on the Linux distribution you're using.
On Debian-Based Systems (Ubuntu, Debian):

- Add Ansible's Official Repository:

```
sudo apt-add-repository ppa:ansible/ansible
```

- Update Package List:

```
sudo apt-get update
```

- Install Ansible:

```
sudo apt-get install ansible
```

On RedHat-Based Systems (CentOS, RedHat):

- Add EPEL Repository:

```
sudo yum install epel-release
```

- Install Ansible:

```
sudo yum install ansible
```

Verifying the Installation

Once installed, you can verify that Ansible is installed correctly by checking its version:

```
ansible --version
```

This command should return the version number, confirming that Ansible is installed and ready to use.

By adding the appropriate repositories, updating the system, and installing the package, you'll have Ansible ready for use on your Linux machine. As we move forward, subsequent chapters will guide you through configuring Ansible, creating playbooks, managing inventory, and much more.

Introduction to YAML

YAML is a human-readable data serialization standard that can be used in conjunction with various programming languages. It's particularly known for its simplicity and ease of understanding, even for those who may not be programmers.

Structure and Syntax

YAML uses indentation to represent nesting and employs simple punctuation marks to indicate lists and key-value pairs. A sample YAML code looks like:

```
name: John Doe
age: 30
skills:
  - Python
  - Ansible
  - DevOps
```

YAML, with its concise yet expressive syntax, offers multiple styles for representing data structures. These styles mainly fall into two categories: Block Style and Flow Style. Understanding these styles is crucial for anyone working with YAML, particularly in Ansible, where YAML is used extensively to define various configurations and tasks.

Block Style

Block Style in YAML relies on indentation and simple punctuation to define the structure. It is often favored for its human readability and simplicity. Below are the key components of Block Style.

Scalars

In YAML, a scalar is a singular value, such as a string or a number. In Block Style, scalars are represented plainly:

```
name: John Doe
age: 30
```

Mappings

Mappings define key-value pairs. Block Style represents mappings with a colon and space:

```
first_name: John
last_name: Doe
```

Sequences

Sequences are lists, and in Block Style, they are represented with dashes:

```
skills:
  - Python
  - Ansible
```

Comments

Comments are preceded by a hash (#) symbol, allowing for annotations:

```
# This is a comment
name: John Doe
```

Multiline Strings

Block Style supports multiline strings using the literal block (|) or folded block (>):

```
description: |
```

Flow Style

Flow Style is more compact and resembles JSON syntax. It allows expressing mappings and sequences in a single line, making it suitable for brief expressions. Following is a closer look at Flow Style.

Scalars

Scalars in Flow Style are similar to Block Style, represented without any quotes, unless necessary:

```
name: "John Doe"
age: 30
```

Mappings

Mappings in Flow Style use curly braces and commas:

```
{ first_name: "John", last_name: "Doe" }
```

Sequences

Sequences use square brackets in Flow Style:

```
skills: ["Python", "Ansible"]
```

Combining Mappings and Sequences

Flow Style allows combining mappings and sequences, providing a concise expression:

```
- { name: "John", skills: ["Python", "Ansible"] }
```

Block vs. Flow Styles

- Readability Aspect: When it comes to human readability, especially in documents with complex structures, the Block Style is often the preferred choice due to its clear and structured format. Flow Style, in contrast, is recognized for its brevity and succinctness.
- Flexibility in Usage: The Block Style excels in handling multiline strings and offers better support for complex nesting. Flow Style, conversely, is more efficient for shorter, more straightforward expressions.
- Interchangeability Feature: Both Block and Flow Styles are interchangeable in their application. They can be used individually or in combination within the same YAML document, offering versatility in document structuring.

Complex Data Types

YAML also supports more complex structures:

Timestamps

YAML can recognize timestamps in various formats:

```
date: 2002-12-14
```

Multiline Strings

YAML offers two styles for multiline strings: Literal (|) and Folded (>):

```
description: |  # Literal Style
  This is a long
  multiline string.

description: >  # Folded Style
  This is a long
  multiline string.
```

Custom Tags

YAML allows the definition of custom tags to define data types specific to the application:

```
!point { x: 10, y: 20 }
```

YAML's various data types offer a powerful means of expressing complex data structures in a concise and human-readable way. From basic scalars like strings and numbers to more complex types like timestamps and custom tags, YAML provides the tools to represent data in diverse and flexible ways. The depth and flexibility of YAML's data types contribute to its wide adoption across various domains, including automation with Ansible.

Write My First YAML Script

In the previous section, after an in-depth exploration of YAML's syntax, styles, and data types, it's time to apply this knowledge to create a sample YAML script. This below example will allow you to verify your understanding of YAML and see how these concepts come together in practice.

Imagine we're working on an Ansible playbook that automates the configuration of a web server. This YAML script will include various aspects of YAML like scalars, sequences, mappings, multiline strings, and more.

```yaml
---
# Ansible Playbook for Web Server Configuration
- hosts: webservers
  vars:
    server_port: 80
    document_root: "/var/www/html"
    enable_ssl: false

  tasks:
    - name: Install Apache HTTP Server
      apt:
        name: apache2
        state: present

    - name: Configure Apache
      template:
        src: /path/to/apache2.conf
        dest: /etc/apache2/apache2.conf

    - name: Enable SSL if required
      block:
        - name: Enable Apache SSL module
          command: a2enmod ssl

        - name: Restart Apache
          service:
            name: apache2
            state: restarted
      when: enable_ssl
```

```
  - name: Deploy Website Content
    copy:
      src: /path/to/website/
      dest: "{{ document_root }}"

handlers:
  - name: Restart Apache
    service:
      name: apache2
      state: restarted
```

This above example demonstrates how the various elements of YAML come together to define a complex structure, in this case, an Ansible playbook for web server configuration.

Configure Ansible

Now that Ansible is installed, it's essential to configure it properly for its first use. Setting up Ansible involves configuring communication with the target machines, defining inventory, and, if needed, customizing Ansible's behavior through configuration files. Given below is how you can set up Ansible for the first time:

Configure Ansible Hosts File (Inventory)

Ansible communicates with remote machines listed in a file called the inventory. You can define an inventory file at /etc/ansible/hosts or any location of your choice. Let us take a simple example of a simple inventory file:

```
[webservers]
web1.example.com
web2.example.com

[databases]
db1.example.com
```

In the above script, [webservers] and [databases] are groups containing the target hosts.

Setup SSH Keys (For SSH Communication)

Ansible usually communicates with remote machines through SSH. Setting up key-based authentication simplifies this communication:

On the control node (your machine running Ansible), generate an SSH key pair:

```
ssh-keygen
```

Then, copy the public key to the remote hosts:

```
ssh-copy-id user@web1.example.com
ssh-copy-id user@web2.example.com
```

Replace user with the appropriate username on the target machines.

Customize Ansible Configuration

You may customize Ansible's behavior by editing the configuration file. The default location is /etc/ansible/ansible.cfg, or you can create a custom ansible.cfg in your project directory.

Example of configuration changes:

```
[defaults]
inventory = /path/to/custom/inventory.ini
remote_user = myuser
```

Test the Configuration

You can check that everything is set up correctly by attempting to connect to your hosts using the ping module:

```
ansible all -m ping
```

If everything is configured correctly, you'll see success messages from all hosts in your inventory.

Keep in mind that Ansible's configurability allows it to adapt to various environments and needs, and you may refer to official Ansible documentation for more advanced configurations tailored to your specific requirements.

Configuration File

Overview

The Ansible configuration file plays a vital role in determining how Ansible behaves when connecting and interacting with hosts. It allows users to customize various settings to tailor Ansible's functionality to their specific needs and preferences. We shall delve into the details of what the configuration file is, how to create one, and what kind of data it can contain.

The Ansible configuration file sets global settings that affect how Ansible functions across all playbooks and tasks. These settings include things like the default inventory file, remote user, privilege escalation methods, timeouts, and much more.

There are various locations where Ansible looks for the configuration file:

- ANSIBLE_CONFIG environment variable (if set)
- ansible.cfg in the current directory
- ~/.ansible.cfg in the user's home directory /etc/ansible/ansible.cfg

To create an Ansible configuration file, you can simply open a text editor and save a new file named ansible.cfg. You can place this file in the current working directory if it's specific to a particular project or in your home directory for user-specific settings.

Given below is how to create an empty configuration file using a terminal text editor like vim:

```
vim ansible.cfg
```

Sample Configuration File

Below is a sample configuration file with explanations for various settings. It's a simple example to showcase some of the common parameters you might want to configure:

```
[defaults]
inventory = /path/to/inventory.ini       # Path to the inventory file
remote_user = myuser                     # Default remote user
private_key_file = /path/to/private.key  # SSH private key
host_key_checking = False                # Disable SSH host key checking
timeout = 30                             # SSH timeout in seconds
retry_files_enabled = False              # Disable retry files
command_warnings = True                  # Enable command warnings
```

```
roles_path = /path/to/roles            # Path to roles directory

[privilege_escalation]
become = True                          # Enable privilege escalation
become_method = sudo                   # Method for privilege escalation
become_user = root                     # User to become
become_ask_pass = False                # Don't ask for password

[ssh_connection]
pipelining = True                      # Enable SSH pipelining
```

The above sample illustrates how you can define different parameters in the configuration file to control various aspects of Ansible's behavior.

Ansible Inventories

Inventories are a crucial component in Ansible's automation engine. They define the hosts and groups of hosts upon which commands, modules, and tasks in a playbook operate. Ansible uses these inventories to identify the machines it must manage, allowing for precise targeting of different devices within a network or cloud environment.

Overview

An inventory is essentially a list of nodes or hosts that Ansible will manage. It can be as simple as a list of IP addresses or as complex as a structured file with variables, attributes, and nesting of hosts within groups.

There are two primary types of inventories in Ansible: static and dynamic.

Static Inventories

Static inventories are the most common type of inventory and are typically defined in an INI-like format or YAML format.

INI-like Format

```
[web]
web1.example.com
web2.example.com
```

```
[db]
db1.example.com
db2.example.com
```

YAML Format

```
web:
  hosts:
    web1.example.com:
    web2.example.com:

db:
  hosts:
    db1.example.com:
    db2.example.com:
```

In these examples, the hosts are categorized into groups (web and db), allowing you to target specific types of servers with your playbooks.

Dynamic Inventories

Dynamic inventories allow Ansible to pull inventory information from external sources, such as cloud providers, LDAP, Cobbler, and more. This is especially useful in environments where servers are constantly being created and destroyed, making static inventory management cumbersome.

A dynamic inventory script can be written in any language (such as Python) and must return a JSON object that describes the hosts, groups, and variables.

Example of Dynamic Inventory JSON Output:

```
{
  "web": {
    "hosts": ["web1.example.com", "web2.example.com"]
  },
  "db": {
```

```
    "hosts": ["db1.example.com", "db2.example.com"]
  }
}
```

Groups and Subgroups

In addition to specifying individual hosts, inventories in Ansible also allow the creation of groups and subgroups. This provides even more structure, letting you define playbooks that target hosts at various levels of granularity.

Example with Subgroups:

```
[web]
web1.example.com
web2.example.com

[db]
db1.example.com
db2.example.com

[production:children]
web
db
```

Variables in Inventories

You can also define variables within an inventory, applying them either to individual hosts or entire groups. These variables can then be referenced within your playbooks and roles.

Example with Variables:

```
[web]
web1.example.com http_port=80
web2.example.com http_port=8080

[web:vars]
nginx_version=1.14
```

Working with Multiple Inventories

Ansible allows you to use multiple inventory files, providing additional flexibility. You can specify different inventories for different environments, such as development, testing, and production. Inventories in Ansible provide a powerful mechanism for managing hosts in a structured and flexible way. By understanding static and dynamic inventories, groups and subgroups, variables, and multiple inventory files, you can wield Ansible's capabilities to suit complex and ever-changing environments. This understanding forms the foundation of effective automation with Ansible, enabling precise control over the diverse elements of a modern IT landscape.

Write Custom Inventory

Writing a custom inventory file in Ansible provides the flexibility to define hosts, groups, variables, and more according to the specific needs and structure of your environment. You can create custom inventories in both static and dynamic formats, tailoring them to fit different scenarios. Following is a demonstration to writing a custom inventory file:

Writing Static Inventory File

INI-like Format

An INI-like format is the simplest way to create a custom inventory file. Following is a step-wise walkthrough to creating one:

- Define Hosts: List individual hosts, either by IP address or hostname.
- Organize into Groups: Organize the hosts into logical groups, such as web servers, database servers, etc.
- Assign Variables: If needed, you can assign variables to individual hosts or groups.

Example:

```
[web]
web1.example.com
web2.example.com

[db]
db1.example.com db_port=5432

[db:vars]
```

```
db_user=admin
```

YAML Format

The YAML format provides a more structured way to define a static inventory. The same elements – hosts, groups, and variables – are used but in YAML's more nested structure.

Example:

```
all:
  children:
    web:
      hosts:
        web1.example.com:
        web2.example.com:
    db:
      hosts:
        db1.example.com:
      vars:
        db_port: 5432
        db_user: admin
```

Writing Dynamic Inventory File

Dynamic inventories are used when your infrastructure is constantly changing, like in a cloud environment. You can write a custom script to fetch the inventory from various sources.

Choose a Programming Language

You can write the script in a language like Python, Ruby, etc., as long as it returns a JSON object.

Fetch Host Information

Gather the host information from your source, like a cloud provider's API.

Format the JSON Object

Construct a JSON object that adheres to Ansible's expected format, including hosts, groups, and variables.

Provide Execution Permissions

Ensure the script has execution permissions, as Ansible will need to run it to fetch the inventory.

Example Python Script:

```
#!/usr/bin/env python

import json

inventory = {
  "web": {
    "hosts": ["web1.example.com", "web2.example.com"]
  },
  "db": {
    "hosts": ["db1.example.com"],
    "vars": {
      "db_port": 5432,
      "db_user": "admin"
    }
  }
}

print(json.dumps(inventory))
```

You can combine multiple static and dynamic inventory files by placing them in a directory and pointing Ansible to that directory. Ansible will merge them together, allowing for a hybrid approach that can handle complex scenarios.

You can further fine-tune your custom inventory by using various parameters and options such as ansible_host, ansible_port, ansible_user, etc. These parameters allow you to specify connection details on a per-host basis.

```
[web]
web1.example.com ansible_host=192.168.1.10 ansible_port=22
```

Writing a custom inventory file in Ansible, whether static or dynamic, allows for a high degree of customization and control over the hosts and groups that Ansible manages. By understanding the formats and options available, you can create a tailored inventory that fits your unique infrastructure and automation needs. This ability to customize inventories is one of the many features that make Ansible a powerful and flexible tool for managing complex systems.

Ansible Ad-hoc Commands

Ad-hoc commands in Ansible represent a powerful and efficient way to execute one-off tasks across your IT infrastructure without the need for writing extensive playbooks. These commands are invaluable to system administrators and DevOps professionals for performing essential tasks on remote machines with simplicity and speed.

Ad-hoc commands in Ansible are single-line instructions designed to perform a specific function. These commands are ideal for occasional tasks or quick tests, offering a straightforward approach to task execution. The commands are executed using Ansible's command-line tool, providing immediate action and feedback.

Gathering Information

One of the primary uses of ad-hoc commands is to collect data about your systems, which is crucial for auditing and troubleshooting.

Example: Check Host Uptime

```
ansible all -m command -a "uptime"
```

This command runs the "uptime" command on all hosts to check how long they have been running.

File Transfer

Ad-hoc commands can be used to transfer files between systems.

Example: Copy a File to Remote Hosts

```
ansible all -m copy -a "src=/local/file.txt dest=/remote/file.txt"
```

This command copies a file from the local machine to all remote hosts.

Package Management

Managing software packages across various hosts can be done effectively with ad-hoc commands.

Example: Install a Package

```
ansible all -m apt -a "name=nginx state=present" -b
```

This command installs the nginx package on all Debian-based hosts.

User Management

Creating, modifying, or deleting user accounts on remote systems is another common task.

Example: Create a User

```
ansible all -m user -a "name=john state=present" -b
```

This command creates a user named "john" on all hosts.

Managing Services

Starting, stopping, or restarting services can be done with ease.

Example: Restart a Service

```
ansible all -m service -a "name=nginx state=restarted" -b
```

This command restarts the nginx service on all hosts.

Working with Files and Directories

Ad-hoc commands can be used to manage files and directories.

Example: Create a Directory

```
ansible all -m file -a "path=/path/to/directory state=directory" -b
```

This command creates a directory on all hosts.

Managing Network Devices

You can even manage network devices with specific modules.

Example: Execute a Command on a Cisco Router

```
ansible routers -m ios_command -a "commands='show ip interface brief'"
```

This command retrieves information from Cisco routers in the group "routers."

Targeting Specific Hosts and Groups

You can direct your commands to specific hosts or groups by changing "all" to the desired group or host pattern.

For example:

```
ansible web -m command -a "uptime"
```

This command would run only on the hosts in the "web" group.

Ad-hoc commands in Ansible represent a crucial aspect of its functionality, offering a flexible and powerful method for executing quick tasks across your infrastructure. These commands are not just limited to file management, user administration, or package handling; they extend to sophisticated network device management and more, making them an indispensable tool in a dynamic IT environment.

Summary

In this chapter, we explored various essential aspects of Ansible, beginning with custom inventory files, which can be created in both static and dynamic formats. Custom inventories offer the ability to define hosts, groups, variables, and more, allowing for tailored environments that fit individual infrastructure needs. We also delved into dynamic inventories, where custom scripts fetch the inventory from sources like cloud providers, offering adaptability in changing environments.

The exploration continued with ad-hoc commands, one of Ansible's powerful features that allow for quick one-off tasks without writing a playbook. Ad-hoc commands cover a wide range of functionalities, including gathering system information, file transfer, package and user management, service control, file and directory operations, and even managing network devices. These commands are executed using the Ansible command-line tool, providing flexibility and efficiency for various common administrative tasks.

Lastly, the chapter underscored how ad-hoc commands can be tailored to specific tasks by using different modules, specifying target hosts and groups, running commands as different users, and specifying extra variables. From managing files to controlling services, ad-hoc commands offer an uncomplicated and effective way to handle many daily tasks in a dynamic IT environment. This information equips professionals with practical knowledge to utilize Ansible's features in real-world scenarios, offering a foundation for more advanced automation techniques.

CHAPTER 2: PLAYBOOKS AND TASKS

Introduction to Playbooks

Playbooks are one of the core features of Ansible and represent the automation engine's heart and soul. They are expressed in YAML format, and this simplicity and clarity make them easily understandable even for those who are new to Ansible. In this chapter, we'll dive deep into what playbooks are, their structure, and how they prove to be an invaluable tool in infrastructure automation.

Playbooks are Ansible's configuration, deployment, and orchestration language. They allow you to describe automation tasks in a very human-friendly way. Think of them as the scripts that tell Ansible what actions to take on what hosts.

Structure

A playbook contains one or more "plays." Each play maps a group of hosts to well-defined roles, representing the tasks to be performed by that role on the particular hosts.

Following is a simple example of a playbook structure:

```
---
- hosts: webservers
  tasks:
    - name: Ensure nginx is installed
      package:
        name: nginx
        state: present

- hosts: databases
  tasks:
    - name: Ensure PostgreSQL is installed
      package:
        name: postgresql
        state: present
```

In the above sample program, there are two plays – one targeting web servers, another targeting database servers.

Tasks

Tasks are the building blocks of playbooks. Each task represents an action to be performed, such as installing a package, starting a service, or creating a file.

Handlers

Handlers are special kinds of tasks that only run when notified by another task. They are typically used to restart services after a configuration change.

Variables

Variables allow you to customize playbooks, making them reusable and adaptable to different environments or user needs.

Benefits

Code Reusability

One of the most significant benefits of Ansible Playbooks is the ability to reuse code. This feature allows you to write a playbook once and then apply it across various environments. This reusability significantly reduces duplication of effort, saving time and resources. For instance, a playbook written for setting up a web server can be reused across development, testing, and production environments with little to no modification. This not only streamlines the deployment process but also ensures consistency across environments.

Human-readable Format

The use of YAML (YAML Ain't Markup Language) in Ansible Playbooks makes them exceptionally user-friendly. YAML's straightforward, text-based format is easy to understand and edit, even for those who are not familiar with programming. This readability is crucial for teams where members might have varying levels of technical expertise. The clarity of the format also helps in reducing errors during playbook creation and makes the review process more efficient.

Flexibility

Flexibility is another key benefit of Ansible Playbooks. They can range from simple tasks, like installing a single package, to complex sequences that manage the entire configuration of a system. This includes managing cloud resources, container orchestration, network devices, and more. This level of flexibility means that playbooks can be adapted to almost any scenario in IT infrastructure and application deployment, making them a versatile tool for a wide range of operations.

Collaboration and Version Control

Playbooks can be integrated into version control systems, such as Git. This integration facilitates collaboration among team members, allowing multiple people to work on the same playbook, track changes, and rollback if necessary. This version control capability is essential for maintaining the integrity of playbooks over time. Moreover, playbooks serve as a form of documentation, providing a clear description of the desired state and configuration of systems. This documentation aspect is particularly valuable in ensuring new team members can understand and contribute to ongoing projects quickly.

Error Handling and Recovery

Error handling is an integral part of any automation tool, and Ansible Playbooks excel in this area. They provide mechanisms to handle errors gracefully, allowing for recovery actions or a clean failure process. This feature is crucial in maintaining system stability and ensuring that automation does not introduce more problems than it solves. For example, if a playbook encounters an issue while configuring a server, it can be designed to revert changes, log the error, and halt the execution, thereby preventing the propagation of the issue.

Integration

Ansible Playbooks can easily integrate with a variety of other tools, expanding their functionality and versatility. This includes integration with cloud services, monitoring systems, and CI/CD pipelines. For instance, a playbook can be set up to interact with cloud APIs to provision and manage cloud resources or to trigger builds and deployments in a continuous integration environment. This level of integration allows Ansible to fit seamlessly into a wide range of IT workflows and processes, enhancing overall efficiency and effectiveness.

Scalability

Playbooks are inherently scalable, making them suitable for managing a few servers or scaling up to thousands. This scalability is particularly beneficial for growing businesses and complex projects that require managing large-scale infrastructures. Playbooks ensure that the same level of control and automation is maintained regardless of the size of the environment they are managing.

Security and Compliance

In an era where security and compliance are paramount, Ansible Playbooks provide mechanisms to enforce security policies and compliance standards. They can automate the deployment of security patches, configuration of firewalls, and other security-related tasks, ensuring that the infrastructure complies with the necessary standards and regulations.

Cost Efficiency

By automating repetitive and time-consuming tasks, playbooks reduce the need for manual intervention, thereby saving on labor costs. Additionally, the reduction in errors and downtime further contributes to cost savings, making Ansible Playbooks a cost-effective solution for IT automation.

Continuous Monitoring and Reporting
Ansible Playbooks can be configured to continuously monitor systems and generate reports, providing insights into the health and status of the infrastructure. This ongoing monitoring is crucial for proactive maintenance and can help in identifying potential issues before they escalate.

The benefits of code reusability, human-readable format, flexibility, collaboration, error handling, integration, scalability, security, cost efficiency, and continuous monitoring make them an invaluable resource for any organization looking to optimize its IT infrastructure.

My First Playbook

Creating your first playbook in Ansible is an exciting step into the world of automation. Here, we'll walk through a practical example to illustrate how to construct a playbook that sets up a basic web server using Apache on a Linux host.

Determine Scenario

For this demonstration, let's consider a scenario where you are responsible for setting up Apache web servers on a group of Linux hosts. You want to automate this process to ensure that it's repeatable, efficient, and error-free.

Identify Steps

Before writing the playbook, it's good to outline the steps required to accomplish the task. For our scenario, we need to:

- Ensure that Apache is installed.
- Ensure that Apache is configured properly.
- Ensure that Apache is running and enabled on boot.

Writing Playbook

Now, we shall translate those steps into Ansible tasks. Create a file named webserver.yml and open it in your favorite text editor. The content of the playbook would look something like this:

```
---
- name: Setup Apache Web Server
  hosts: webservers
  become: yes

  tasks:
```

```
  - name: Ensure Apache is installed
    package:
      name: apache2
      state: present

  - name: Ensure Apache configuration file is in place
    template:
      src: /path/to/apache2.conf.j2
      dest: /etc/apache2/apache2.conf
    notify: restart apache

  - name: Ensure Apache service is running and enabled
    service:
      name: apache2
      state: started
      enabled: yes

handlers:
  - name: restart apache
    service:
      name: apache2
      state: restarted
```

Running Playbook

Once the playbook is ready, you can run it using the following command:

```
ansible-playbook webserver.yml
```

While doing so, you may keep certain best practices in mind such as,

- Always name your tasks; this makes the playbook more readable.
- Test your playbook on a non-production environment first.
- Use variables for values that might change between different environments or users.

- Consider using roles if your playbook becomes very complex, to separate different concerns.

This particular playbook takes a clear, structured approach to automate the process of setting up Apache web servers on Linux hosts. It showcases fundamental Ansible concepts like tasks, handlers, and privilege escalation, offering a solid foundation for more complex scenarios.

Tasks in Ansible

Purpose

Tasks are the fundamental building blocks in Ansible playbooks, defining the actions that need to be executed on the target hosts. Each task represents a single operation, such as installing a package, copying a file, or restarting a service. They provide a mechanism to articulate the desired state of a system, encapsulating the actions necessary to achieve that state.

Tasks serve several vital purposes in Ansible:

- They are the means to automate repetitive operations, ranging from simple actions like updating a file to complex orchestration like rolling updates across a cluster.
- Tasks are written in a declarative manner, describing the desired state rather than the steps to achieve it. This makes them more natural to write, read, and maintain.
- Tasks can be bundled into roles and reused across different playbooks, promoting code reuse and consistency.
- They provide mechanisms to handle failures, retries, and conditional execution, enabling robust and resilient automation.

Types of Tasks

Regular Tasks

Regular tasks are the most common type of tasks and define the basic actions to be performed. An example would be:

```
- name: Install Nginx
  package:
    name: nginx
    state: present
```

Conditional Tasks

Conditional tasks are executed based on specific conditions using the when clause. They provide a way to make decisions based on variables, system facts, or outputs of other tasks.

```
- name: Install Apache on Debian systems
  package:
    name: apache2
    state: present
  when: ansible_facts['os_family'] == "Debian"
```

Looping Tasks

Looping tasks are used to iterate over a list of items and perform a task for each item. They provide an efficient way to handle repetitive actions.

```
- name: Install multiple packages
  package:
    name: "{{ item }}"
    state: present
  with_items:
    - git
    - curl
    - vim
```

Asynchronous Tasks

Asynchronous tasks are used to run tasks in the background, providing a way to perform long-running operations without blocking the playbook execution.

```
- name: Start a long-running task
  command: /path/to/long_running_script.sh
  async: 600
  poll: 0
```

Notification and Handlers

Tasks can notify handlers, which are special tasks triggered by other tasks. This allows for efficient execution of actions like restarting a service only if its configuration has changed.

```
- name: Update Apache config
  template:
    src: apache.conf.j2
    dest: /etc/apache2/apache2.conf
  notify: Restart Apache

handlers:
  - name: Restart Apache
    service:
      name: apache2
      state: restarted
```

Blocks

Blocks allow grouping tasks together, which can be particularly useful for error handling and conditional execution.

```
block:
  - name: Task 1
    ...
  - name: Task 2
    ...

rescue:
  - name: Handle failure
    ...
```

Task Execution

Running Tasks

Executing tasks in Ansible is an essential part of the automation workflow. Not only is it about running the tasks to achieve the desired state, but also about validating them to ensure they perform as expected. Given below is how to execute and validate tasks in Ansible.

Running Playbooks

Tasks are executed by running Ansible playbooks. A playbook is a YAML file containing one or more plays, where each play consists of a set of tasks to be run on specified hosts.

```
ansible-playbook my_playbook.yml
```

Limiting Hosts

You can limit the execution to specific hosts using the --limit option:

```
ansible-playbook my_playbook.yml --limit host1,host2
```

Specifying Inventory File

If you need to use a different inventory file, use the -i option:

```
ansible-playbook my_playbook.yml -i my_inventory.ini
```

Running Specific Tasks

Use tags to run specific tasks within a playbook:

```
- name: Install Nginx
  package:
    name: nginx
    state: present
  tags:
    - install
```

Then run the playbook with:

```
ansible-playbook my_playbook.yml --tags install
```

Validating Tasks

Validation is crucial for ensuring that tasks perform as expected. Several techniques allow you to validate tasks in Ansible.

Dry-Run (Check Mode)

You can run a playbook in check mode using the --check option. It simulates the run, showing you what changes would be made without actually making them:

```
ansible-playbook my_playbook.yml --check
```

Using Assertions

Assertions allow you to perform checks to validate the state. Following is an example:

```
- name: Assert that Nginx is installed
  assert:
    that:
      - "'nginx' in ansible_facts.packages"
    fail_msg: "Nginx is not installed"
    success_msg: "Nginx is installed"
```

Validating Configuration Files

You can use the validate parameter with the template or copy module to validate configuration files:

```
- name: Validate Apache config
  template:
    src: apache2.conf.j2
    dest: /etc/apache2/apache2.conf
    validate: "apachectl -t -f %s"
```

Debugging Tasks

Use the debug module to print debug information, helping in validating variables or expressions:

```
- name: Debug example
  debug:
    msg: "The value of my_variable is {{ my_variable }}"
```

Using Handlers

Handlers are special tasks triggered by notifications from other tasks. They can be used for validation steps like restarting a service after a configuration change.

Monitoring and Logging

Keeping track of task execution is vital for troubleshooting and auditing. Ansible provides detailed logs and integrates with monitoring tools.

Verbose Output

Use the -v option to get more detailed output:

```
ansible-playbook my_playbook.yml -vvv
```

Logging Configuration

You can configure Ansible to log to a file by setting up logging in the Ansible configuration file.

Executing and validating tasks in Ansible encompasses more than simply running a playbook. It involves understanding the mechanisms that control execution, the tools and techniques for validation, and the practices for monitoring and logging. This multi-faceted approach ensures that your automation is not only effective but also reliable and maintainable.

Organize Tasks and Playbooks

Organizing tasks and playbooks in Ansible becomes crucial as complexity grows in your infrastructure automation. Good organization ensures maintainability, scalability, and collaboration among team members. Following is a detailed practical walkthrough on how to structure your tasks and playbooks for complex scenarios.

Organizing Tasks

Using Roles

Roles provide a framework for organizing tasks, handlers, files, templates, and variables:

```
roles:
  - role: webserver
    vars:
      http_port: 80
```

Task Dependencies

You can manage dependencies between tasks using the include_tasks directive or by specifying dependencies in roles.

Using Tags

Tags allow you to run specific parts of a playbook:

```
tasks:
  - name: Install package
    package:
      name: nginx
    tags: [ 'install' ]
```

Organizing Playbooks

Splitting Playbooks into Multiple Files

Large playbooks can be broken down into smaller files using the include or import_playbook directives.

Playbook Directories and Naming Conventions

Create directories to categorize playbooks, like provisioning/, deployments/, etc., and follow a clear naming convention.

Variable Files

Use variable files to separate the variable definitions from task logic:

```
vars_files:
  - vars/main.yml
```

Reusable Playbooks

Create playbooks that can be reused across different environments by parameterizing them.

To sum up, organizing tasks and playbooks in Ansible is not merely about keeping things tidy, rather it is about creating a scalable and maintainable automation environment, especially in complex scenarios.

Errors & Troubleshooting

Working with tasks and playbooks in Ansible can sometimes lead to errors or unexpected behavior. Understanding these common errors and knowing how to troubleshoot them is an essential skill for anyone working with Ansible.

Syntax Errors

YAML Syntax Errors

YAML syntax errors are often due to improper indentation, missing colons, or incorrect usage of dashes. YAML, being a sensitive format, requires strict adherence to its syntax rules.

Solution: Tools like yamllint are invaluable in validating YAML files, helping detect and correct syntax errors. Regular use of such tools can save significant time and prevent runtime errors.

Ansible-Specific Syntax Errors

These errors occur when Ansible modules are used incorrectly or variables are referenced improperly.

Solutions: Running ansible-playbook with the --syntax-check option is a proactive approach to catch these errors early. This option parses the playbook and checks for basic syntax mistakes, ensuring that the playbook is syntactically correct before execution.

Connection Errors

SSH Connection Issues

SSH connection problems can include authentication failures and host key verification issues.

Solution: Checking SSH configurations, verifying credentials, and ensuring proper permissions are essential steps in resolving these issues. SSH connection errors are often straightforward to solve but can be disruptive if overlooked.

Network Issues

Network-related errors might manifest as unreachable hosts or complications due to firewall settings.

Tools like ping or traceroute are useful in troubleshooting network connectivity. Ensuring that there are no network blockages or misconfigurations that prevent Ansible from reaching the target hosts is crucial.

Task Execution Errors

Permission Errors

Execution of a task without the required privileges leads to permission errors.

Solution: Utilizing Ansible's become feature allows privilege elevation for specific tasks, mitigating permission issues.

Module Errors
Absence of necessary packages or libraries for a particular module leads to errors.

Solution: Ensuring that all dependencies of a module are installed and updated is a key step in preventing these errors.

Item Idempotency Errors
Non-idempotent tasks may produce inconsistent results over multiple runs.

Solution: Writing tasks to be idempotent, where repeated executions yield the same results, is fundamental in maintaining consistency and reliability.

Variable and Templating Errors

Undefined Variables
Common Issues: Errors arise when a playbook references a variable that has not been defined.

Solution: Ensuring proper variable definition and using default filters (e.g., variable | default(value)) can prevent these errors.

Templating Errors
Common Issues: Incorrect Jinja2 templating syntax or flawed logic can cause execution errors.

Solution: Rigorous testing of templates and adherence to Jinja2 syntax best practices are critical in mitigating these issues.

Role and Dependency Errors

Role Not Found
An error occurs if a role specified in a playbook is absent.

Solution: Verifying the existence and correct path of the role is essential to resolving this issue.

Unresolved Dependencies
Missing task or playbook dependencies can lead to errors.

Solution: Proper definition and inclusion of all required dependencies are necessary to ensure smooth playbook execution.

Error Handling in Ansible

Ansible offers several mechanisms to handle errors gracefully:

Using Blocks

The block, rescue, and always structure in Ansible allows for defining a set of tasks and their error handling mechanisms. For example:

```
block:
  - name: task 1
    command: ...
rescue:
  - name: handle failure
    debug:
      msg: "An error occurred."
```

Ignoring Errors

Specific errors can be ignored using the ignore_errors directive, allowing a playbook to continue execution even when a task fails.

By adhering to syntax best practices, employing built-in error handling, and utilizing debugging features, Ansible users can create robust automation solutions. These solutions not only gracefully handle errors but also continue to function effectively, ensuring reliability and efficiency in diverse IT environments.

Sample Program: Deploying Web Application on Multiple Servers

We shall consider a real-world scenario where we need to configure multiple web servers to host a website. We'll perform the following tasks:

- Install the necessary software packages (e.g., Apache, PHP).
- Configure Apache with the proper settings.
- Deploy the website's static content to the web servers.
- Restart the Apache service to apply changes.
- Verify that the website is accessible.

We'll create a multi-task playbook for deploying a web application across multiple Linux servers. The playbook will handle the installation and configuration of Apache, PHP, and deployment of the website files. We'll also include a task to check the website's accessibility after deployment.

```yaml
- name: Deploy Web Application
  hosts: webservers
  become: yes
  vars:
    apache_config_file: /etc/httpd/conf/httpd.conf
    website_files_path: /var/www/html
    website_url: http://localhost

  tasks:
    - name: Install Apache
      package:
        name: httpd
        state: present

    - name: Install PHP
      package:
        name: php
        state: present

    - name: Configure Apache
      lineinfile:
        path: "{{ apache_config_file }}"
        line: "IncludeOptional sites-enabled/*.conf"

    - name: Deploy website files
      copy:
        src: /path/to/local/website/files/
        dest: "{{ website_files_path }}"
        mode: '0755'

    - name: Restart Apache service
      service:
        name: httpd
```

```
      state: restarted

  - name: Check website accessibility
    uri:
      url: "{{ website_url }}"
      status_code: 200
    register: website_status

  - name: Report website status
    debug:
      msg: "Website is accessible."
    when: website_status.status == 200
```

To execute the playbook, you must have an inventory file that lists the target servers under the [webservers] group.

Given below is an example inventory file, inventory.ini:

```
[webservers]
server1.example.com
server2.example.com
```

Then you can execute the playbook using the following command:

```
ansible-playbook -i inventory.ini deploy_website.yml
```

This command will apply the playbook to the servers listed under the "webservers" group in the inventory file. The tasks will be executed in sequence, installing the required software, configuring Apache, deploying the website files, restarting the Apache service, and verifying the website's accessibility.

Summary

This chapter took us on a journey through Ansible playbooks, starting with a fundamental understanding of their role in automating repetitive tasks. Written in YAML, playbooks are essential for scripting complex, multi-action procedures in Ansible, offering a dynamic platform for defining a sequence of actions to be executed across various hosts. The essence of automation in Ansible lies in these playbooks, which allow for parameterization and sharing of intricate task sequences. We learned the process of crafting a basic playbook, applying it to a real-world example to demonstrate how playbooks address practical challenges in software management and deployment.

We then delved deeper into the realm of Ansible tasks, exploring their objectives and the diverse types they encompass within a playbook. Each task in Ansible signifies an individual step or action, such as installing software or managing services. The chapter equipped us with practical know-how on crafting and implementing these tasks, covering a range of scenarios from straightforward to complex. Furthermore, we explored common pitfalls encountered when working with tasks and playbooks, along with effective strategies for troubleshooting and resolving these issues.

In the final part, we amalgamated the learned concepts to construct a comprehensive playbook capable of orchestrating a web application's deployment across numerous servers. This step-wise walkthrough showcased the formulation of a playbook, articulation of varied tasks, and their strategic arrangement. Implementing the playbook brought to life an automated process for a web application's setup, encompassing installation, configuration, deployment, and validation stages. This intricate example underscored Ansible's robustness and adaptability in infrastructure management, affirming the pivotal role of playbooks in devising scalable and reusable automation strategies.

CHAPTER 3: WORKING WITH MODULES

What are Ansible Modules?

Definition

Modules in Ansible are at the core of its automation capabilities, acting as discrete units that perform specific tasks. They encapsulate the logic needed to carry out certain actions, whether it's manipulating files, managing packages, or interacting with network devices. We shall delve into the nature, function, and applications of modules in Ansible, focusing on their role in IT automation and DevOps.

Modules in Ansible are small programs that do the actual work in your playbook, such as managing services, installing packages, or creating files. They are designed to be resource-driven, meaning that they manage the state of something, whether present or absent. Ansible contains hundreds of built-in modules that are maintained by the community, enabling users to perform common tasks without having to write any code.

Function of Modules

A module takes arguments and returns JSON data. This interaction is processed by the Ansible engine, which then takes appropriate actions on the managed nodes. When you run a playbook, Ansible sends these modules to the remote hosts, along with the arguments defined in your playbook, and executes them.

- Resource State Management: Modules enforce the desired state of resources. For example, the "file" module ensures that a file has the correct permissions and ownership.

- Action Execution: Modules execute actions on remote hosts. For example, the "command" module runs a given command on the target system.

- Information Gathering: Some modules, like the "setup" module, gather information about the system, such as OS distribution, hardware details, etc.

How Modules Work?

Firstly, these modules are designed to be executed on remote hosts. This execution can occur in two primary ways: either directly through ad-hoc commands for quick, one-off tasks or within playbooks for more complex, multi-step workflows. This flexibility allows Ansible to adapt to a variety of automation scenarios, whether it's a simple task or a part of a larger orchestrated plan.

A key feature of most Ansible modules is their Idempotency. This means that running a module multiple times under the same conditions will not change the outcome after its first successful execution. Idempotent modules are smart enough to make changes only when the current state of the system doesn't align with the desired state specified in the module. This attribute is crucial for maintaining consistency and reliability in automated environments, ensuring that scripts and commands do not inadvertently alter systems in unexpected ways.

Lastly, integrating these modules within playbooks is a straightforward process, thanks to Ansible's use of simple YAML syntax. This integration allows for a seamless blend of various modules within a single playbook, enabling complex automation tasks to be scripted and executed efficiently. The ease of calling modules within playbooks underscores Ansible's user-friendly design, making it accessible even to those who might not have extensive programming experience.

Applications of Modules

For Configuration Management, modules are instrumental in ensuring that systems are configured accurately and efficiently. They handle various aspects such as managing configuration files and services, which is fundamental in maintaining system integrity and performance.

In the Continuous Integration/Continuous Deployment (CI/CD) pipeline, modules facilitate the automation of testing and deployment processes. This capability is a cornerstone in DevOps, supporting a seamless and efficient workflow for code integration and deployment.

Network Automation is another area where modules prove invaluable. Network-specific modules aid in the configuration and management of network devices, simplifying what used to be complex and manual network management tasks.

When it comes to Security Compliance, security-focused modules come into play. They are designed to enforce security policies and ensure that systems adhere to various compliance standards, a critical aspect in today's cybersecurity-conscious environment.

In Cloud Management, cloud-specific modules provide the functionality to interact with various cloud service providers. These modules make it possible to automate the provisioning and management of cloud resources, an essential feature in the age of cloud computing.

Some common modules that are widely used across these applications include:

- File Management: Modules like file, copy, and template are used for managing files across systems.
- Package Management: Modules such as apt and yum cater to the management of software packages in different environments.
- Service Management: The service and systemd modules are key in managing system services, ensuring they are running as required.
- User Management: For handling user accounts and groups, modules like user and group are employed.

These examples highlight the versatility and breadth of modules in Ansible, showcasing their integral role in automating various aspects of IT operations and DevOps workflows.

Core Modules in Ansible

Core modules in Ansible are fundamental to its functionality, providing essential capabilities to manage resources, interact with systems, and orchestrate tasks. We shall delve into some of the key core modules, explaining their functions, and providing examples to illustrate how they can be employed.

File Management

file

The file module manages files, directories, and symlinks. It can be used to set permissions, ownership, and other file attributes.

Example:

```
- name: Ensure a directory exists
  file:
    path: /etc/my_app
    state: directory
    mode: '0755'
    owner: root
    group: root
```

copy

The copy module copies files from the local system to the remote system.

Example:

```
- name: Copy a configuration file
  copy:
    src: /local/path/to/file.conf
    dest: /etc/my_app/file.conf
```

template

The template module renders a template file on the local system and copies it to the remote system.

Example:

```
- name: Deploy a template file
  template:
    src: /local/templates/file.j2
    dest: /etc/my_app/file.conf
```

Package Management

apt

The apt module is used for managing packages on Debian-based systems.

Example:

```
- name: Install nginx
  apt:
    name: nginx
    state: present
```

yum

The yum module manages packages on RedHat-based systems.

Example:

```
- name: Remove httpd
  yum:
    name: httpd
    state: absent
```

Service Management

service

The service module controls services on remote hosts.

Example:

```
- name: Restart nginx
  service:
    name: nginx
    state: restarted
```

systemd
The systemd module interfaces with the systemd system manager on Linux.

Example:

```
- name: Enable and start sshd
  systemd:
    name: sshd
    enabled: yes
    state: started
```

User Management

user
The user module manages user accounts.

Example:

```
- name: Create a user
  user:
    name: john
    group: developers
    home: /home/john
```

group
The group module manages groups.

Example:

```
- name: Create a group
```

```
  group:
    name: developers
    gid: 5000
```

Network Modules

net_interface

The net_interface module manages network interfaces.

Example:

```
- name: Enable eth0 interface
  net_interface:
    name: eth0
    state: up
```

These core modules provide comprehensive functionality for various automation tasks within Ansible. They abstract the complexity of managing resources, allowing the user to perform a wide range of actions using simple YAML syntax. By understanding these core modules and their applications, administrators and DevOps professionals can create powerful and flexible automation workflows, tailoring them to suit their specific needs and environments.

Cloud Modules

In addition to the previously learned modules, Ansible's cloud modules enable seamless interaction and management of cloud resources, spanning various cloud providers. These modules simplify the complex tasks associated with cloud orchestration, scaling, and provisioning.

We shall explore some of the popular cloud modules, providing examples for each.

Amazon Web Services (AWS) Modules

ec2

As mentioned earlier, the ec2 module manages Amazon EC2 instances.

Example:

```
- name: Launch an EC2 instance
  ec2:
```

```
    instance_type: t2.micro
    key_name: mykey
    image: ami-12345678
    region: us-west-2
```

s3

The s3 module handles operations with Amazon S3 buckets.

Example:

```
- name: Create an S3 bucket
  s3_bucket:
    name: my-bucket
    region: us-west-2
```

rds

The rds module manages Amazon RDS instances.

Example:

```
- name: Create an RDS instance
  rds:
    db_instance_identifier: mydb
    engine: MySQL
    instance_type: db.m4.large
```

Microsoft Azure Modules

azure_rm_virtualmachine

The azure_rm_virtualmachine module creates and manages virtual machines in Azure.

Example:

```
- name: Create a VM
  azure_rm_virtualmachine:
    resource_group: myResourceGroup
```

```
    name: myVM
    vm_size: Standard_DS1_v2
    admin_username: adminUser
```

azure_rm_storageaccount
This module manages Azure Storage Accounts.

Example:

```
- name: Create a storage account
  azure_rm_storageaccount:
    name: mystorageaccount
    resource_group: myResourceGroup
```

Google Cloud Platform (GCP) Modules

gcp_compute_instance
The gcp_compute_instance module creates and manages Compute Engine instances.

Example:

```
- name: Create a Compute Engine instance
  gcp_compute_instance:
    name: my-instance
    zone: us-central1-a
    machine_type: n1-standard-1
```

Gcp_storage_bucket
This module manages Google Cloud Storage buckets.

Example:

```
- name: Create a storage bucket
  gcp_storage_bucket:
    name: my-bucket
    location: US
```

OpenStack Modules

os_server

The os_server module manages OpenStack compute instances.

Example:

```
- name: Launch an instance
  os_server:
    name: my-instance
    image: ubuntu
    flavor: m1.tiny
```

Os_network

This module manages OpenStack networking.

Example:

```
- name: Create a network
  os_network:
    name: my-network
```

VMware Modules

vmware_guest

The vmware_guest module manages VMs in VMware environments.

Example:

```
- name: Create a VM
  vmware_guest:
    hostname: vcenter.mydomain.com
    folder: /Datacenter/vm
    name: myVM
    guest_id: centos64Guest
    datacenter: Datacenter
```

vmware_vm_inventory
This module gathers information about VMs in a VMware environment.

Example:

```
- name: Get VM inventory
  vmware_vm_inventory:
    hostname: vcenter.mydomain.com
    username: user
    password: pass
```

These cloud modules encapsulate the diverse functionalities offered by different cloud providers. By using them, IT and DevOps professionals can automate, orchestrate, and manage cloud resources in a vendor-agnostic manner, leveraging Ansible's simplicity and robustness.

Network Modules

Networking is an essential aspect of modern IT systems, and Ansible offers a variety of modules to automate and manage network devices across multiple vendors. These network modules facilitate configuration, management, and troubleshooting. Following is a detailed examination of some key network modules:

Cisco Modules

ios_command
The ios_command module enables you to execute arbitrary commands on Cisco IOS devices.

Example:

```
- name: Show version
  Ios_command:
commands: show version
```

ios_banner
This module manages the login banner on Cisco IOS devices.

Example:

```
- name: Set login banner
```

```
  ios_banner:
    banner: login
    text: "Authorized Access Only!"
```

Juniper Junos Modules

junos_command

This module sends arbitrary commands to Juniper Junos devices.

Example:

```
- name: Show version
  Junos_command:
commands: show version
```

junos_banner

Manages the banner on Juniper devices.

Example:

```
- name: Set login banner
  junos_banner:
    banner: login
    text: "Authorized Users Only!"
```

Arista EOS Modules

eos_command

Executes arbitrary commands on Arista EOS devices.

Example:

```
- name: Show interfaces
  Eos_command:
commands: show interfaces
```

VyOS Modules

vyos_command

This module executes arbitrary commands on VyOS devices.

Example:

```
- name: Show configuration
  vyos_command:
 commands: show configuration
```

F5 BIG-IP Modules

bigip_command

Executes arbitrary commands on F5 BIG-IP devices.

Example:

```
- name: Show system version
  Bigip_command:
 commands: show sys version
```

bigip_pool

This module manages connection pools on BIG-IP.

Example:

```
- name: Create a pool
  bigip_pool:
    name: my-pool
    lb_method: round-robin
```

Nokia SR-OS Modules

sros_command

The sros_command module sends arbitrary commands to Nokia SR-OS devices.

Example:

```
- name: Show system information
  Sros_command:
 commands: show system information
```

Fortinet FortiOS Modules

fortios_system_banner
Manages the login banner on Fortinet devices.

Example:

```
- name: Configure banner
  fortios_system_banner:
    login_banner: "Authorized Access Only!"
```

Huawei CloudEngine Modules

ce_command
Executes arbitrary commands on Huawei CloudEngine devices.

Example:

```
- name: Display version information
  Ce_command:
 commands: display version
```

These network modules provide ability to automate repetitive tasks enables teams to focus on strategic objectives, innovate, and adapt to ever-changing business needs and technology landscapes.

Custom Modules

Writing custom Ansible modules allows for a level of flexibility and control that can cater to specific automation requirements. While Ansible has a plethora of built-in modules for various purposes, creating a custom module may be necessary to integrate unique or proprietary systems.

In the given below, we'll outline the process of writing a custom module, focusing on a practical example: a module to manage firewall rules.

Let's say you need to automate the management of firewall rules in a proprietary firewall system that doesn't have pre-built Ansible modules. You have an API available that allows you to list, create, update, and delete rules.

Choosing Programming Language

Ansible modules can be authored in any language capable of returning JSON data, with Python being a popular choice due to its rich library support and ease of integration with Ansible's utilities.

Creating Module File

Begin by creating a Python file for your custom module, for example, firewall_rule.py. This file will house the code for your module.

You'll need the basic Ansible module utilities. Start by importing the necessary libraries:

```
#!/usr/bin/python
from ansible.module_utils.basic import AnsibleModule
import requests
```

Defining Module Arguments

Next, define the parameters your module will accept. For managing firewall rules, this might include the rule's name, action, source, destination, and protocol:

```
def main():
    module = AnsibleModule(
        argument_spec=dict(
            name=dict(required=True),
            action=dict(choices=['allow', 'deny'], required=True),
            source=dict(required=True),
            destination=dict(required=True),
            protocol=dict(choices=['tcp', 'udp'], required=True),
        )
    )
```

Implementing Logic

The core of your module is the logic that interacts with the firewall system's API. For instance, to create a new rule, define a function like create_rule:

```
def create_rule(module):
    url = "http://firewall/api/rules"
    headers = {"Content-Type": "application/json"}
    payload = {
        "name": module.params['name'],
        "action": module.params['action'],
        "source": module.params['source'],
        "destination": module.params['destination'],
        "protocol": module.params['protocol']
    }
    response = requests.post(url, json=payload, headers=headers)

    if response.status_code == 201:
        module.exit_json(changed=True)
    else:
        module.fail_json(msg="Failed to create rule", response=response.text)
```

Calling Function

Within the main() function, invoke the create_rule function to execute the module's primary action:

```
    create_rule(module)
```

Executing Main Function

Finally, call the main() function at the end of the script:

```
if __name__ == '__main__':
    main()
```

You can now use this custom module in an Ansible playbook like any built-in module:

```
- name: Create firewall rule
  firewall_rule:
    name: "Allow HTTP"
```

```
  action: "allow"
  source: "0.0.0.0/0"
  destination: "192.168.1.1"
  protocol: "tcp"
```

Testing and Debugging

Ensure to test the module thoroughly and add error handling as required.

By following this process, you can write custom Ansible modules that fit specific requirements of your IT automation tasks. Remember that extensive testing and validation are critical for production use.

Build Custom Modules

Creating and testing custom Ansible modules requires a systematic approach to ensure that they meet the desired requirements and function reliably. We'll continue with the firewall rule example and cover the process of building and testing the custom module.

Setting up the Environment

First, you need a development environment where you can write and test the code. You'll require:

- A Python environment.
- Ansible installed.
- Access to the firewall system's API (or a simulated environment).

Writing Custom Module

Continuing from the previous steps, we shall refine the module code by adding more functions to manage the firewall rules, such as updating and deleting.

Updating Rule

```
def update_rule(module, rule_id):
  url = f"http://firewall/api/rules/{rule_id}"
  headers = {"Content-Type": "application/json"}
  payload = {
    "name": module.params['name'],
    "action": module.params['action'],
```

```
        "source": module.params['source'],
        "destination": module.params['destination'],
        "protocol": module.params['protocol']
    }
    response = requests.put(url, json=payload, headers=headers)

    if response.status_code == 200:
        module.exit_json(changed=True)
    else:
        module.fail_json(msg="Failed to update rule", response=response.text)
```

Deleting Rule

```
def delete_rule(module, rule_id):
    url = f"http://firewall/api/rules/{rule_id}"
    response = requests.delete(url)

    if response.status_code == 200:
        module.exit_json(changed=True)
    else:
        module.fail_json(msg="Failed to delete rule", response=response.text)
```

Testing Functions

Now that you have the functions defined, you'll need to integrate them within the main() function and add conditional logic to perform create, update, or delete operations based on the parameters passed.

Creating Test Playbooks

Develop Ansible playbooks that utilize the custom module, each covering a different aspect of the module's functionality.

Example: Creating a Rule

```
- name: Create firewall rule
```

```
  firewall_rule:
    name: "Allow HTTP"
    action: "allow"
    source: "0.0.0.0/0"
    destination: "192.168.1.1"
    protocol: "tcp"
```

Example: Updating a Rule

```
- name: Update firewall rule
  firewall_rule:
    rule_id: 123
    name: "Allow HTTPS"
    action: "allow"
    source: "0.0.0.0/0"
    destination: "192.168.1.1"
    protocol: "tcp"
```

Finally, write comprehensive documentation that explains how to use the module, including examples and explanations of parameters.

The process of creating and testing a custom Ansible module is an iterative and methodical one, requiring a mix of development skills, understanding of Ansible, and domain knowledge of the system being managed (in this case, a proprietary firewall system). Following this approach, you can develop robust and reliable custom modules that integrate seamlessly with Ansible's ecosystem.

Errors & Troubleshooting

Working with Ansible modules, particularly when developing custom modules, involves complexities that can lead to errors or unexpected behavior. Here, we will explore some of the common pitfalls and strategies for handling them, continuing from the example of the custom firewall module.

Parameter Validation Errors

Failing to validate input parameters correctly can lead to runtime errors. For example, if a required parameter is missing or an incorrect data type is passed.

Solution

Use Ansible's built-in parameter validation within the module to enforce rules.

Example:

```
module = AnsibleModule(
    argument_spec=dict(
        name=dict(type='str', required=True),
        action=dict(type='str', choices=['allow', 'deny'], required=True),
        source=dict(type='str', required=True),
        ...
    )
)
```

API Communication Errors

Communication with external APIs may fail due to network issues, incorrect endpoints, or authentication errors.

Solution

Handle exceptions that arise from network calls and provide detailed error messages to the user.

Example:

```
try:
    response = requests.put(url, json=payload, headers=headers)
except requests.exceptions.RequestException as e:
    module.fail_json(msg=str(e))
```

Invalid State Errors

If the module does not handle the current state of the system correctly, it can attempt to perform invalid operations, such as deleting a non-existent firewall rule.

Solution

Always check the current state and make decisions based on it.

Example:

```
def delete_rule(module, rule_id):
    # Check if the rule exists
    existing_rule = get_rule_by_id(module, rule_id)
    if not existing_rule:
        module.fail_json(msg=f"Rule with ID {rule_id} does not exist.")
    ...
```

Idempotency Errors

Ansible modules should be idempotent, meaning that repeated executions with the same parameters should have the same outcome. Failure to achieve this can cause unpredictable behavior.

Solution

Ensure that the module checks the current state and only makes changes if necessary.

Example:

```
def update_rule(module, rule_id):
    existing_rule = get_rule_by_id(module, rule_id)
    if existing_rule['action'] == module.params['action']:
        module.exit_json(changed=False)
    ...
```

Debugging Challenges

Debugging custom modules can be difficult without proper logging and error messages.

Solution

Implement detailed logging within the module and provide clear and informative error messages.

Example:

```
import logging
logging.basicConfig(filename='module.log', level=logging.DEBUG)
```

```
def update_rule(module, rule_id):
    logging.debug(f"Updating rule with ID {rule_id}")
    ...
```

Dependency Errors

Modules may depend on specific libraries or system configurations that are not available on the target system.

Solution

Ensure that dependencies are documented, and if possible, include checks within the module to verify their presence.

Example:

```
try:
    import requests
except ImportError
    module.fail_json(msg="The requests library is required.")
```

Handling errors gracefully not only improves the user experience but also simplifies troubleshooting and maintenance. The code snippets above, tailored to the ongoing firewall rule management example, showcase practical solutions for each of these challenges.

Summary

In the beginning of this chapter, we delved into the fundamentals of Ansible modules, exploring their function, applications in IT automation and DevOps, and the integral role they play in tasks and playbooks. We explored different types of modules including core, cloud, and network modules, with an emphasis on how they simplify complex automation tasks by encapsulating functionalities and interfaces. Through detailed examples, we demonstrated the use and importance of these different module categories in modern infrastructure management.

As the chapter evolved, our focus shifted towards the development of custom modules. We guided you through a real-world scenario, covering the stages of writing, constructing, and testing a custom module. This practical approach shed light on the nuances of creating tailored modules to meet specific needs. We outlined crucial steps such as parameter definition, API interaction, and managing system states, providing a clear and practical insight into custom module development.

Towards the end of the chapter, we tackled the common challenges and pitfalls encountered in module development, along with strategies to overcome them. Topics like parameter validation, API communication, handling invalid states, ensuring idempotency, debugging, and managing dependencies were learned in detail. The chapter was enriched with specific solutions and code examples for each type of error, empowering you to create resilient and robust Ansible modules. This comprehensive examination of error handling, combined with the continuous example, reinforced best practices in Ansible module development.

Chapter 4: Roles, Files, and Templating

Introduction to Roles

In this chapter, we'll focus on the concept of roles within Ansible, a central aspect of automation that adds structure, reusability, and efficiency to playbooks.

Roles in Ansible are a way to organize tasks and related content, allowing you to automate routine actions in a streamlined and standardized manner. They can be thought of as pre-packaged automation procedures, containing tasks, handlers, templates, and other supporting components that work together to achieve a specific outcome.

Why Roles?

Roles are an essential aspect of Ansible for several reasons:

- Modularity - Roles offer a modular approach to organizing automation content. By breaking down complex automation tasks into smaller, more manageable pieces, roles make code easier to understand and maintain. This modularity is critical in creating a structured and organized automation environment, where each component has a specific purpose and function. It allows developers and system administrators to isolate different parts of a process, making the overall system more robust and easier to debug.
- Reusability - One of the greatest advantages of using roles in Ansible is their reusability. Roles can be used across various projects and environments, ensuring consistency and efficiency in the automation process. This reusability also means that once a role is developed, it can be shared and reused in different scenarios, reducing the need to rewrite code for common tasks. This not only saves time but also helps in maintaining a standardized approach across different projects and teams.
- Abstraction - Roles allow for the abstraction of complex logic. By encapsulating specific logic within a role, they provide a cleaner and more simplified interface for users. This level of abstraction is beneficial in managing complexity, as users can interact with a role without needing to understand the intricate details of the tasks it performs. It allows for a more user-friendly approach to automation, where the focus can be on the higher-level operations rather than the underlying specifics.
- Version Control - Version control is another significant aspect of roles in Ansible. Roles can be version-controlled, which enables the tracking of changes, collaboration among team members, and an easier process for rollback if necessary. This is particularly important in a team environment where multiple people may be working on the same project. Version control ensures that changes are tracked and managed efficiently, reducing the risk of conflicts and errors.

Roles vs. Tasks and Modules

While tasks define a single automation step in Ansible, roles provide a higher level of organization. Tasks are the building blocks used within roles, executing specific actions like installing a package or starting a service. Modules are the underlying tools that tasks utilize to perform these actions. They can be simply summarized as below:

- Tasks: Simple, single-purpose automation steps.
- Modules: Pre-built or custom tools utilized by tasks to perform specific functions.
- Roles: Collections of tasks, variables, files, templates, and modules organized to perform a broader, more complex operation.

Structure of Roles

Roles in Ansible are typically composed of several directories, each serving a distinct purpose in the automation process:

- tasks: The main list of tasks that the role will execute.
- handlers: Special tasks that respond to notifications from other tasks.
- templates: Template files that will be deployed by this role.
- files: Files that need to be deployed without changes.
- vars: Variables associated with the role.

Creating and using Roles

The process of creating a role in Ansible involves setting up the aforementioned structure and populating it with the necessary tasks, templates, handlers, and other components. Once created, roles can be easily called within a playbook. This enhances the readability and reusability of the playbook, as roles can encapsulate complex logic and functionality, simplifying the main playbook structure.

The utilization of roles in playbooks brings a level of organization and clarity that is essential for managing large and complex automation tasks. By abstracting the complexity into roles, the main playbook becomes more streamlined and easier to understand. This approach not only improves the maintainability of the code but also allows for greater collaboration among team members, as each role can be developed, tested, and maintained independently.

Create Roles

We shall proceed with the exploration of Ansible roles by taking a more hands-on approach when it comes to the creation of different roles. We are going to refer back to the scenario that we learned earlier, which involves automating the process of setting up a web server environment that includes a database. The installation of a web server, the creation of a database, and the configuration of firewalls are all examples of distinct roles that will be required for this scenario.

Organizing Roles

We'll create three distinct roles for this scenario:

- web_server: To install and configure the web server.
- database: To set up the database system.
- firewall: To set up the firewall rules.

Creating Web Server Role

Directory Structure:

```
web_server/
  tasks/
    main.yml
  templates/
    httpd.conf.j2
  vars/
    main.yml
```

Tasks (web_server/tasks/main.yml):

```
---
- name: Install Apache
  yum:
    name: httpd
    state: present

- name: Configure Apache
  template:
    src: httpd.conf.j2
    dest: /etc/httpd/conf/httpd.conf
  notify: Restart Apache
```

```yaml
- name: Enable and start Apache
  systemd:
    name: httpd
    state: started
    enabled: true
```

Variables (web_server/vars/main.yml):

```yaml
---
http_port: 80
```

Template (web_server/templates/httpd.conf.j2):

```
Listen {{ http_port }}
```

Creating Database Role

We'll follow a similar structure for the database role:

Directory Structure:

```
database/
  tasks/
    main.yml
```

Tasks (database/tasks/main.yml):

```yaml
---
- name: Install MySQL
  yum:
    name: mysql-server
    state: present

- name: Enable and start MySQL
  systemd:
```

```
  name: mysqld
  state: started
  enabled: true
```

Creating Firewall Role

The firewall role might look like:

Directory Structure:

```
firewall/
  tasks/
    main.yml
```

Tasks (firewall/tasks/main.yml):

```
---
- name: Open HTTP port
  firewalld:
    port: 80/tcp
    permanent: true
    state: enabled

- name: Reload firewalld
  command: firewall-cmd --reload
```

Using Roles in Playbook

Finally, you would utilize these roles within a playbook by referencing them:

```
---
- hosts: webservers
  roles:
    - web_server
    - database
    - firewall
```

By organizing the automation into roles, we've broken down a complex task into reusable, scalable components. This approach promotes maintainability and allows for more manageable adjustments in the future.

Use of Roles

We shall take what we learned from the previous example and put it into practice by carrying out the roles that were defined. You will learn how to use the roles of web_server, database, and firewall by going through this in-depth walkthrough. These roles were defined in the previous section.

Creating Main Playbook

First, we need to create the main playbook where these roles will be called. We shall call this playbook site.yml. This playbook will apply the roles to a specific group of servers, named webservers.

site.yml:

```
---
- hosts: webservers
  become: yes
  roles:
    - web_server
    - database
    - firewall
```

This playbook states that it will run on hosts under the webservers group and includes three roles: web_server, database, and firewall. The become: yes ensures that the playbook is executed with root permissions.

Defining Inventory File

Roles need to know on which hosts they will be applied. You'll specify this in an inventory file.

inventory.ini:

```
[webservers]
server1.example.com
Server2.example.com
```

This file defines a group called webservers, consisting of two servers.

Running Playbook

Once the playbook and inventory are ready, you can execute the playbook using the ansible-playbook command:

```
ansible-playbook -i inventory.ini site.yml
```

In some cases, roles may have dependencies on other roles. These dependencies can be defined in a meta/main.yml file within the role directory.

For example, within the web_server role, you could create:

web_server/meta/main.yml:

```
---
dependencies:
  - firewall
```

This signifies that the web_server role depends on the firewall role, ensuring the firewall rules are set up before the web server is configured.

Overriding Role Variables

If you want to override the variables defined within a role, you can do so in the playbook:

site.yml:

```
---
- hosts: webservers
  become: yes
  roles:
    - role: web_server
      vars:
        http_port: 8080
    - database
    - firewall
```

This would override the http_port variable within the web_server role to 8080.

Including/Excluding Specific Roles

You might want to run only a specific role or exclude certain roles during playbook execution. You can use tags for this purpose.

site.yml:

```
---
- hosts: webservers
  become: yes
  roles:
    - role: web_server
      tags: web
    - role: database
      tags: db
    - role: firewall
      tags: firewall
```

Run only the web role:

```
ansible-playbook -i inventory.ini site.yml --tags web
```

By using the roles as defined above, you can create robust and maintainable automation code that can be easily adapted to different environments and use cases.

File Management

Managing files and directories is an essential aspect of any automation tool, and Ansible provides powerful modules to handle different file operations. In the context of the previous example, involving a web server, we'll explore various file management tasks that you might encounter in real-world scenarios. We'll be using Ansible's file, copy, template, and lineinfile modules.

Creating Directories

First, we might need to create directories to store our web server's files and logs.

roles/web_server/tasks/main.yml:

```
- name: Ensure web server directories are present
  file:
    path: "{{ item }}"
    state: directory
    mode: '0755'
  with_items:
    - /var/www/html
    - /var/log/web_server
```

Copying Files

Next, we may need to copy static files like images, CSS, or JavaScript.

roles/web_server/tasks/main.yml:

```
- name: Copy static assets to web server directory
  copy:
    src: files/assets/
    dest: /var/www/html/assets/
```

Managing Configuration Files with Templates

We often need to create configuration files based on variables, and the template module lets us do this.

For instance, the web server's main configuration file might need to vary depending on the environment (staging, production, etc.).

roles/web_server/templates/web_server.conf.j2:

```
server {
    listen {{ web_server_port }};
    root {{ web_server_root }};
    # ...
}
roles/web_server/tasks/main.yml
```

```
- name: Configure web server
  template:
    src: web_server.conf.j2
    dest: /etc/web_server/conf.d/web_server.conf
```

Modifying Existing Files with lineinfile

Sometimes we need to modify existing files, perhaps to update a configuration setting. The lineinfile module is perfect for these tasks.

roles/web_server/tasks/main.yml:

```
- name: Ensure the correct timezone in PHP configuration
  lineinfile:
    path: /etc/php.ini
    regexp: '^date.timezone ='
    line: 'date.timezone = UTC'
```

Managing File Permissions

Ensuring correct permissions is crucial for security.

roles/web_server/tasks/main.yml:

```
- name: Set permissions for web server directories
  file:
    path: "{{ item }}"
    mode: '0750'
    owner: www-data
    group: www-data
  with_items:
    - /var/www/html
    - /var/log/web_server
```

Removing Files

Lastly, there might be scenarios where you need to delete files or directories.
roles/web_server/tasks/main.yml:

```
- name: Remove unused directory
  file:
    path: /var/www/old_directory
    state: absent
```

The combination of these Ansible modules allows for comprehensive management of files and directories within the automation scripts. In the context of a web server, these tasks cover common operations such as creating directories, copying files, templating configurations, managing permissions, and cleaning up unnecessary files.

Ansible Templates

Templates are a central part of Ansible's power and flexibility. They allow users to manage complex configurations by enabling the customization of files using variables. In Ansible, templates use the Jinja2 templating engine, but we'll focus exclusively on the concept and use of templates without delving into Jinja2 specifics.

Functionalities

In the context of Ansible, a template is a file that includes placeholders for variables. These placeholders are replaced with actual values when the template is executed, creating a file tailored to a specific host, group of hosts, or other criteria.

- Parameterization: Templates enable you to parameterize configuration files. Rather than having multiple nearly identical files, you can create one template with variables that get filled in when the template is used.
- Reuse: Templates promote the reuse of code. By creating a template, you can define a configuration that can be used across multiple systems or environments, replacing specific variables as needed.
- Dynamic Content Generation: Templates can take advantage of Ansible's facts and variables to create content that's specific to a host or environment. This means you can create files that are tailored to the specific attributes of the system they are deployed on.
- Integration with Other Ansible Features: Templates can be used in conjunction with other Ansible features such as roles and playbooks. This enables seamless integration and promotes modular design.

Benefits

- Simplification - Templates can dramatically simplify configuration management. By defining a single template for a configuration file, you can reduce duplication and make changes more manageable. Altering a configuration across multiple systems or environments might require a single change to a template, rather than editing numerous individual files.
- Consistency - Templates promote consistency by ensuring that the same logic and structure are applied wherever the template is used. This minimizes the risk of human error and inconsistencies in configuration that can lead to problems.
- Scalability - With templates, scaling becomes more manageable. Whether you are managing ten systems or ten thousand, templates enable you to maintain uniform configuration across all of them. You can quickly deploy changes across a vast infrastructure by merely modifying the template.
- Customization - Templates allow for customization on a per-host or per-group basis, enabling you to tailor configuration files to the specific needs of different systems or environments. You can create generic templates that become highly specific when filled with the relevant variables.
- Collaboration - Templates help in collaboration among team members. By having a standard template, team members can work on different parts of an infrastructure without conflicts and with clear understanding.

Imagine managing a fleet of web servers with different domains, ports, and document roots. Rather than creating a separate configuration file for each server, you can create a template containing variables for these settings.

```
server {
  listen {{ web_server_port }};
  server_name {{ domain }};
  root {{ document_root }};
}
```

Then, using Ansible's capabilities, you can deploy this template to each server, substituting the appropriate values for each variable. This single template can serve an entire fleet of web servers, each with its unique configuration. By encapsulating configuration logic into templates and utilizing variables for customization, Ansible provides a scalable, maintainable, and consistent way to manage configurations.

Up and Running with Jinja2

Jinja2 is a modern and designer-friendly templating engine for Python programming language. It's often used within Ansible templates to transform data inside a template expression ({{ }}) and expose it to a playbook or role. Here, you'll be introduced to the basics of Jinja2 and how to use it in conjunction with Ansible for your IT automation and DevOps needs.

Jinja2 Features

Jinja2 comes from a family of text-based templating languages and is inspired by Django's template engine. It has some key characteristics:

- Template Inheritance - One of the standout features of Jinja2 is its support for template inheritance. This feature allows developers to create a base "skeleton" template that contains all the common elements and structure used across different web pages or configurations. Other templates can then "inherit" this base structure and override specific sections as needed. This approach greatly reduces redundancy in template creation, as common elements like headers, footers, and navigation bars need to be defined only once. It leads to cleaner, more maintainable code and significantly speeds up the development process.

- Filters - Jinja2 filters are another powerful feature. Filters are used to modify the contents of variables within template expressions. They provide functionalities similar to traditional programming transformations or formatting operations. For instance, filters can be used to format dates, convert strings to uppercase or lowercase, apply mathematical transformations, and more. This feature enhances the flexibility and expressiveness of templates, allowing for more dynamic and responsive content generation.

- Macros - Macros in Jinja2 function similarly to functions in conventional programming languages. They allow for the definition of reusable pieces of code within templates. Macros can take arguments and return results, just like functions. This feature is especially useful for repetitive tasks within templates, as it enables code reuse, leading to more concise and readable templates.

- Control Structures - Jinja2 supports various control structures, such as if-statements and for-loops. These structures introduce logic into templates, enabling the creation of more dynamic and interactive content. For instance, a for-loop can be used to iterate over a list of items and render each item in HTML. If-statements can be used to conditionally display content based on certain criteria. This inclusion of programming logic in templates allows for a high degree of customization and flexibility in content rendering.

In Ansible, Jinja2 templates are used to generate host files dynamically or to do something based on the value of variables or facts. The basic syntax for expressions is {{ some_variable }}, which gets evaluated and replaced with the value of some_variable.

Variables and Expressions

You can use variables and expressions inside double curly braces:

```
message: "Welcome to {{ platform }}"
```

Filters

Jinja2 filters allow data manipulation and can be used in conjunction with variables:

```
{{ some_variable | default('Default Value') }}
```

The filters in Jinja2 transform variables and can be used for various purposes:

- default: Provides a default value if a variable is undefined.
- length: Returns the length of a string or list.
- to_json: Converts data into JSON format.
- regex_replace: Performs a regular expression replace operation.

Conditionals

Conditional statements like if-else can be used inside templates:

```
{% if users %}
  {% for user in users %}
    {{ user.name }}
  {% endfor %}
{% else %}
  No users found.
{% endif %}
```

Loops

You can loop over sequences using the for loop:

```
{% for item in items %}
  {{ item }}
{% endfor %}
```

Macros

Macros are reusable snippets of code:

```
{% macro say_hello(name) %}
 Hello, {{ name }}!
{% endmacro %}
```

Template Inheritance

You can create a base template and then extend it in child templates. This allows for consistent layouts:

```
{% extends "base.html" %}
{% block content %}
 This content replaces the base content block.
{% endblock %}
```

Sample Program: Generate Web Server Configuration

Given below is an example of how you might create a web server configuration file using Jinja2 with Ansible:

Create Template (nginx.conf.j2)

```
server {
   listen {{ web_server_port }};
   server_name {{ domain }};
   root {{ document_root }};
}
```

Create Ansible Playbook

```
---
- name: Configure Nginx
  hosts: webservers
  vars:
    web_server_port: 80
    domain: example.com
    document_root: /var/www/html
  tasks:
    - name: Generate Nginx Configuration
      template:
        src: nginx.conf.j2
        dest: /etc/nginx/sites-available/default
```

This playbook utilizes the Jinja2 template to generate Nginx configuration file tailored to each web server. By leveraging variables, filters, loops, conditionals, and other features, you can create highly customizable automation processes that adapt to the needs of your infrastructure.

Sample Program: Building Ansible Playbook for Web Server

Combining the knowledge of roles, tasks, and templates, we shall build a robust Ansible playbook for a web server. For consistency, we'll continue using the Nginx web server example from previous learnings.

Structuring Project

To structure the project in Ansible, you can break it down into roles. Roles allow you to organize tasks and associated files, templates, and variables.

Following is how you might structure your project:

```
webserver/
├── roles/
│   ├── nginx/
│   │   ├── tasks/
│   │   │   └── main.yml
│   │   ├── templates/
```

```
│ │ │ └── nginx.conf.j2
│ │ └── vars/
│ │     └── main.yml
├── playbook.yml
```

Nginx Role

Under the nginx role, you'll have the following components:

Tasks (tasks/main.yml)

This file contains the tasks required to install and configure Nginx.

```
---
- name: Install Nginx
  apt:
    name: nginx
    state: present

- name: Generate Nginx Configuration
  template:
    src: nginx.conf.j2
    dest: /etc/nginx/sites-available/default

- name: Ensure Nginx is Running
  service:
    name: nginx
    state: started
    enabled: yes
```

Templates (templates/nginx.conf.j2)

This Jinja2 template provides the Nginx configuration.

```
server {
   listen {{ web_server_port }};
   server_name {{ domain }};
```

```
    root {{ document_root }};
}
```

Variables (vars/main.yml)

Variables provide configurable settings for the playbook.

```
---
web_server_port: 80
domain: example.com
document_root: /var/www/html
```

Main Playbook (playbook.yml)

The main playbook incorporates the Nginx role to apply the configuration to your web servers.

```
---
- name: Deploy Web Server
  hosts: webservers
  roles:
    - nginx
```

Once the playbook and role are configured, you can execute the playbook using the command:

```
ansible-playbook playbook.yml
```

With the help of roles, tasks, and templates, you've developed a reusable, atomic procedure for setting up a Nginx web server. Through the use of roles, you are able to encapsulate associated responsibilities, variables, and templates, which encourages reuse across a variety of projects. The utilization of Jinja2 templates makes it possible to achieve dynamic configuration based on the values of variable parameters. You can continue to expand this structure in the real-world scenario by adding more roles, templates, and tasks to manage other aspects of your infrastructure, such as security configurations, user management, and more.

Summary

The intricate components of Ansible were examined in depth in this chapter, with a focus on roles, tasks, templates, and their practical application. In Ansible, roles serve as an important organizational structure, allowing the encapsulation of tasks, variables, and templates into reusable components. The chapter demonstrated how to structure an Ansible project using roles by deploying a Nginx web server, providing a modular and maintainable approach to automation. The use of tasks within roles allows for the concise definition and execution of individual steps, which contributes to the automation process's clarity and precision.

Templates, particularly those based on Jinja2, play an important role in the creation of dynamic configuration files. The chapter demonstrated how to define a web server configuration using Jinja2 templates, which support variable substitution and logical constructs. The use of roles and templates together promotes reusability and adaptability, allowing for the diverse needs of different environments and applications. The chapter expanded understanding of Ansible's capabilities in managing complex IT automation by putting these concepts into practice in a real-world scenario.

The third aspect of learning concentrated on error handling, custom module creation, file management, and complex scenario execution. Following practical demonstrations, the chapter taught the step-by-step process of writing and building custom modules. The role of file management in infrastructure automation was demonstrated with hands-on examples, emphasizing various file operations in the context of web server management. Finally, the chapter integrated all of the roles, tasks, and templates learned, resulting in a multifaceted playbook that combines various Ansible elements. This chapter significantly improved understanding of Ansible's robust features and functionalities in IT automation and DevOps through consistent examples and real-world applications.

CHAPTER 5: MANAGING SYSTEMS WITH ANSIBLE

Ansible for System Administration

System administration refers to the management and maintenance of computer systems and networks. It encompasses a broad spectrum of tasks aimed at ensuring the stability, integrity, and efficiency of system resources. From configuring hardware, installing and maintaining software, to managing user accounts, monitoring system performance, and securing the network, system administration serves as the backbone of any IT environment.

Ansible Responsibilities

The role of a system administrator is multifaceted and dynamic. Key responsibilities include:

- Configuring Hardware - Setting up and maintaining the physical components of a computer network, such as servers, routers, and switches. This involves ensuring that all hardware components are functioning correctly and efficiently.
- Software Installation and Maintenance - System administrators are responsible for installing, updating, and maintaining software applications and operating systems. This task is crucial to ensure that the software on all machines is up-to-date and running smoothly, providing the necessary tools and applications for users.
- User Account Management - Administrators manage user accounts, ensuring secure and efficient access to the network and its resources. This includes creating user accounts, setting permissions, and monitoring usage to maintain security and operational efficiency.
- Monitoring System Performance - Regularly monitoring the performance of the system to ensure it runs at optimal levels. This includes checking for any potential issues that could cause disruptions in service and implementing solutions to mitigate such risks.
- Securing the Network - One of the most critical roles is network security. System administrators implement and maintain security protocols to protect the system from external threats, such as malware or cyber-attacks. They also manage firewalls and other security measures to safeguard data and maintain privacy.

Automation in System Administration

With the advancement of technology, the complexity of IT infrastructures has increased. Modern IT environments often feature a mix of cloud-based services, virtual machines, and distributed networks, adding layers of complexity to the system administration role. This complexity necessitates a more sophisticated approach to managing IT resources, especially in terms of automation and process streamlining.

- Automated Provisioning: Ansible can automate the entire process of setting up physical or virtual servers. This includes configuring hardware settings, partitioning disks, setting up the operating system, and installing necessary software packages.
- Configuration Management: Ansible provides a declarative language to define system configurations. This includes managing user accounts, setting up services, defining firewall rules, and maintaining software versions across different environments.
- Software Deployment: Ansible facilitates the automated deployment of applications. This includes everything from pulling the latest code from a version control system, configuring the environment, compiling code if necessary, and managing dependencies.
- Security Management: Ansible can automate the application of security patches, manage firewall rules, and enforce security policies. It can also be used to regularly audit systems for compliance with security standards.
- Monitoring and Reporting: Ansible can be integrated with monitoring tools to automate health checks and performance monitoring of systems. It can generate reports and alerts, providing insights into system status and potential issues.
- Scaling and Load Balancing: Ansible's dynamic inventory allows it to adapt to changes in the infrastructure, ensuring that load balancing and scaling are handled efficiently. It can automatically add or remove servers based on load, ensuring optimal resource utilization.
- Disaster Recovery: Ansible can automate backup processes and enable streamlined recovery procedures. It can synchronize data across different locations, ensure regular backups, and facilitate quick restoration in the event of a system failure.
- Application Orchestration - Ansible's orchestration capabilities allow for the coordination of different systems, ensuring that complex multi-step tasks are executed in the proper order. This includes starting or stopping services, rolling updates, and coordinated deployments across multiple systems.
- Integrating with Cloud and Virtualization - Ansible supports various cloud providers and virtualization platforms, allowing seamless provisioning and management of virtual machines and cloud resources. Its modular design enables integration with different platforms, ensuring a consistent management experience regardless of the underlying technology.

User and Group Management Overview

User management and group management are foundational concepts in system administration that revolve around controlling access to system resources. We shall break down each aspect to understand their significance in a computing environment.

User Management:

User management involves the creation, modification, and deletion of user accounts within a system. These accounts enable individuals to access resources, run applications, and perform tasks based on their specific permissions.

- Creation: System administrators create user accounts with unique usernames and passwords, defining access levels and associated privileges.
- Modification: Over time, users' roles and permissions may change, requiring updates to their account details.
- Deletion: When a user no longer requires access, their account must be properly deactivated or removed to maintain security.
- Authentication and Authorization: User management ensures that only authenticated users can access authorized resources. This includes mechanisms for password management, multi-factor authentication, and role-based access control.

User management is essential for:

- Security: By controlling who has access to what, user management helps in protecting sensitive information.
- Accountability: By associating actions with specific users, it provides a clear audit trail.
- Usability: Users have personalized access to the tools and information they need, enhancing productivity.

Group Management:

Group management involves creating and managing groups of users. These groups simplify the assignment of permissions by allowing administrators to manage multiple users simultaneously. Instead of assigning permissions to each user individually, administrators can assign permissions to a group, and all members of that group inherit those permissions.

- Creation: Groups are created to represent different roles, departments, or functions within an organization.
- Modification: As needs change, groups may require updates to their membership or permissions.
- Deletion: Unnecessary groups must be deleted to maintain a clean and organized system.

Group management streamlines administration with:

- Efficiency: It's easier and faster to manage permissions for groups rather than individual users.
- Consistency: Ensures that all users within a group have consistent access rights.
- Flexibility: Allows for quick changes in permissions across a set of users by modifying the group's permissions.

In Ansible, user and group management can be automated to ensure consistency, reduce manual errors, and save time. Ansible provides modules like user and group for managing user accounts and groups across different systems. By defining the desired state in a playbook, Ansible can ensure that user and group configurations are consistent across a wide range of environments.

Managing Users and Groups

Managing users and groups is a vital task in system administration. In the context of setting up a web server, this involves creating specific user accounts and groups that have the necessary permissions to manage and run the server. By doing this, you can ensure that only authorized individuals have access to the web server and its underlying system resources.

Below, we'll walk through how to manage users and groups with Ansible, applying them to our previous web server scenario.

Creating User Accounts and Groups

In the Ansible playbook, you can use the user and group modules to create and manage user accounts and groups.

Define User and Group

First, we shall create a user account for managing the web server and a group for all web administrators.

```
---
- hosts: webserver
  become: yes
  tasks:
    - name: Create webadmin group
      group:
        name: webadmin
```

```
    state: present

  - name: Create webuser account
    user:
      name: webuser
      group: webadmin
      create_home: yes
      state: present
```

Here, webadmin is the group responsible for web administration, and webuser is the user account associated with the group.

Configure Permissions

Next, we shall ensure that the webuser has the correct permissions to manage the web server's content directory.

```
  - name: Set permissions for web directory
    file:
      path: /var/www/html
      owner: webuser
      group: webadmin
      mode: '0755'
```

This sets the ownership of the web directory to webuser and the group ownership to webadmin, allowing members of the webadmin group to modify the content.

Manage User Passwords

Secure password management is essential. Ansible can handle password changes, as shown below:

```
  - name: Set password for webuser
    user:
      name: webuser
      password: "{{ 'mysecurepassword' | password_hash('sha512') }}"
```

Adding/Removing Users from Groups

You can add or remove users from groups using the groups parameter in the user module.

```
- name: Add additional users to webadmin group
  user:
    name: "{{ item }}"
    groups: webadmin
    append: yes
  with_items:
    - user1
    - user2
```

Deleting Users and Groups
If needed, users and groups can be removed:

```
- name: Remove obsolete user
  user:
    name: olduser
    state: absent
```

Applying Playbook
After defining the playbook, you can apply it to the target web server using the following command:

```
ansible-playbook webserver.yml
```

Making new user accounts, establishing new groups, adjusting permissions, and managing user membership are all part of managing users and groups in a web server scenario. Ansible provides a straightforward method for automating these tasks, which guarantees that the web server is managed in a secure and efficient manner.

Cron Jobs

When it comes to operating systems that are similar to Unix, Cron jobs are tasks that are scheduled to run automatically at predetermined intervals. They automate repetitive tasks, which ensures that these operations take place at the appropriate time without requiring any intervention from a human being. This makes them an essential component of system administration. When applied to a web server, cron jobs may be utilized for a variety of purposes, including but not limited to monitoring tasks, log rotation, system updates, and periodic backups.

You are able to easily manage cron jobs with the help of Ansible's cron module, which enables the definition, modification, or removal of tasks in a manner that is readable by humans. With the help of examples that are connected to the web server scenario, we will investigate how to create and manage cron jobs with Ansible in the following section.

Exploring Cron Jobs

Cron jobs are defined by a cron table, or crontab, which specifies when a task should run and what command to execute.

A cron job entry consists of six fields:

- Minute (0 - 59)
- Hour (0 - 23)
- Day of the month (1 - 31)
- Month (1 - 12)
- Day of the week (0 - 7; 0 and 7 represent Sunday)
- Command to execute

Creating Cron Jobs

The following example playbook illustrates how you can create a cron job to backup the web server's content directory every day at 3:00 AM:

```
---
- hosts: webserver
  become: yes
  tasks:
    - name: Daily backup of web content
      cron:
        minute: "0"
        hour: "3"
        user: webuser
        job: "/usr/local/bin/backup-web-content.sh"
```

The minute, hour, user, and job parameters define the time, user under which the job runs, and the command to execute.

Modifying Cron Jobs

You can update an existing cron job using the same cron module, changing the parameters as needed. For example, to change the backup time to 4:00 AM:

```
- name: Update backup time to 4:00 AM
  cron:
    minute: "0"
    hour: "4"
    user: webuser
    job: "/usr/local/bin/backup-web-content.sh"
```

Removing Cron Jobs

Cron jobs can be removed by setting the state parameter to absent. Given below is how you might remove the backup job:

```
- name: Remove backup job
  cron:
    user: webuser
    job: "/usr/local/bin/backup-web-content.sh"
    state: absent
```

Complex Scheduling

Cron jobs can be scheduled with more complex timing. For instance, to run a script every 15 minutes during business hours on weekdays:

```
- name: Run script during business hours
  cron:
    minute: "*/15"
    hour: "9-17"
    weekday: "1-5"
    user: webuser
    job: "/usr/local/bin/business-hours-task.sh"
```

Applying Playbook

Finally, run the playbook as usual:

```
ansible-playbook cronjobs.yml
```

Best Practices

- Script Usage: Instead of placing complex commands directly in the cron job, create a script with proper logging and error handling and call it from the cron job.
- Environment Variables: Be aware that cron jobs run with a minimal environment, so specify all necessary paths and variables.
- Permissions: Set proper permissions on scripts called by cron jobs to ensure security.

You will be able to improve the level of automation and reliability in your system if you are able to manage cron jobs using Ansible. The combination of cron jobs and Ansible provides a powerful solution that can be adapted to meet the specific requirements of a web server or other system administration scenarios. This solution can be used for performing routine maintenance, running system health checks, or automating backups.

Sample Program: Automate Workstation Setup

Automating workstation setup is an essential aspect of system administration, especially in large organizations. With Ansible, you can standardize the configuration, ensuring that every workstation has the required software, settings, and security measures. Here, we will explore how to automate a workstation setup, focusing on a generic example that can be adapted to various environments.

Imagine a scenario where you're responsible for setting up workstations for a software development team.

Each workstation needs:

- A specific version of the operating system.
- Development tools (e.g., compilers, text editors, IDEs).
- Version control systems (e.g., Git).
- Network configurations (e.g., proxy settings).
- Security measures (e.g., firewall rules, antivirus).

We will create an Ansible playbook to address these requirements, ensuring that the workstation is ready for development activities.

Define Hosts

Start by defining the hosts that the playbook will target. In your inventory file, you might have a group called [workstations]:

```
[workstations]
workstation1.example.com
Workstation2.example.com
```

OS Configuration

The following playbook tasks can be used to ensure the operating system is up to date:

```
- name: Ensure OS is up to date
  apt:
    update_cache: yes
    upgrade: safe
  when: ansible_os_family == 'Debian'
```

Development Tools

Install the required development tools, such as compilers, text editors, and IDEs:

```
- name: Install development tools
  package:
    name:
      - gcc
      - make
      - vim
      - code # Visual Studio Code
    state: present
```

Version Control Systems

Ensure Git is installed and configured:

```
- name: Install Git
  package:
```

```
    name: git
    state: present

- name: Configure Git
  git_config:
    scope: global
    name: user.name
    value: "Developer"
```

Network Configuration

Set up the necessary network configurations, such as proxy settings:

```
- name: Configure HTTP Proxy
  lineinfile:
    path: /etc/environment
    line: "http_proxy=http://proxy.example.com:8080/"
```

Security Measures

Configure firewall rules and other security measures:

```
- name: Allow SSH and HTTP
  ufw:
    rule: allow
    name: "{{ item }}"
  with_items:
    - ssh
    - http
```

Running Playbook

After defining these tasks in a playbook file (e.g., workstation-setup.yml), you can run the playbook against the workstations:

```
ansible-playbook -i inventory.ini workstation-setup.yml
```

You can extend the example that was presented earlier in accordance with the particular requirements of the organization or team that you are working with. You are able to make the playbook more adaptable and easy to maintain by incorporating variables, templates, and roles into it.

Summary

In the fifth chapter, we learned how to use Ansible as a system administrator, and how it can streamline complicated processes like managing users and groups, setting up workstations, and scheduling cron jobs. Standardization and efficiency are critical in system administration, and Ansible allows administrators to define precisely how systems should be configured, ensuring consistency across diverse environments. You gain a foundational understanding of system administration with Ansible by understanding the fundamental concepts of user and group management, cron jobs, and workstation automation.

Throughout the chapter, practical demonstrations were provided to walk you through concrete examples and scenarios related to web server setup. Manage users and groups, set up workstations with specific OS configurations, development tools, network configurations, version control systems, and security measures were all detailed steps. Cron jobs were explained and demonstrated, demonstrating how they can be used for task scheduling. The hands-on approach enabled you to gain a thorough understanding of how to apply these concepts in real-world scenarios.

This chapter highlighted Ansible's flexibility and robust functionality, demonstrating its applicability in a variety of system administration domains. Complex and repetitive tasks can be automated using modules, playbooks, roles, and templates, increasing productivity and reducing human error. The examples in this chapter can be customized to meet the specific needs of an organization or project and serve as a starting point for more complex configurations. You have gained the skills required to use Ansible's capabilities in a variety of system administration contexts as a result of these exercises.

CHAPTER 6: ANSIBLE IN NETWORKING

Network Automation Overview

What is Network Automation?

Network automation, a key component in the evolving landscape of IT infrastructure, represents a profound shift from traditional, manual network management to a more efficient, programmable, and automated approach. This shift is critical in today's fast-paced business environments, where agility and responsiveness are paramount.

It refers to the process of automating the planning, configuration, management, testing, deployment, and operations of physical and virtual devices within a network. Its scope is broad, encompassing everything from executing simple configuration changes to orchestrating complex workflows and automating entire operational tasks.

Key Elements of Network Automation

We shall explore the key elements of network automation in detail:

Configuration Management

- Automating Configurations – Configuration management automates the process of configuring network devices. This includes initializing device settings, updating firmware, setting up VLANs, routing configurations, and more. By automating these tasks, organizations can ensure that their network configurations are consistent across all devices, reducing the possibility of human error.

- Templates and Policies – Utilizing templates and policies allows for standardized configurations across the network. These templates ensure that each device is configured according to a predefined set of policies and standards, which is crucial for maintaining security and compliance.

- Version Control and Change Management – Keeping track of changes made to configurations is vital. Version control systems can be integrated into the network automation process, allowing network administrators to roll back to a previous configuration if an issue arises. This also aids in auditing and compliance tracking.

- Idempotency – An important aspect of configuration management is idempotency, ensuring that running the same configuration multiple times does not change the result after the first application. This is crucial for maintaining stability in the network infrastructure.

Testing and Validation

- Automated Testing – Network automation includes automated testing of network configurations and infrastructure. This could involve testing for connectivity, bandwidth, latency, or compliance with security policies.
- Continuous Integration/Continuous Deployment – Implementing CI/CD practices allows network teams to test changes in a controlled environment before deploying them to production, reducing the likelihood of network downtime.
- Validation – Post-deployment validation ensures that changes have been applied as intended and that the network is functioning correctly. This can involve automated scripts that check for compliance and operational status.

Deployment

- Automated Provisioning – Deployment in network automation means automatically provisioning network hardware and software. This includes initializing devices, deploying virtual network functions (VNFs), or configuring cloud-based network resources.
- Infrastructure as Code (IaC) – Treating network configurations as code enables network teams to use software development practices for network deployment. This approach allows for repeatable, scalable, and efficient network deployment processes.
- Zero-Touch Provisioning (ZTP) – ZTP allows devices to be configured and updated automatically, without manual intervention, significantly speeding up the deployment process and reducing errors

Operations and Management

- Performance Monitoring – Continuous monitoring of network performance is a critical aspect of network automation. Automated tools can monitor bandwidth usage, latency, packet loss, and other key performance indicators to ensure the network operates at optimal levels.
- Event-Driven Automation – Network operations can be automated based on specific events or triggers. For instance, if a device fails, a backup device can be automatically brought online.
- Issue Resolution – Automating the process of issue detection and resolution can significantly enhance network reliability. For example, if a performance metric falls below a certain threshold, an automated script could be triggered to rectify the issue.
- Maintenance and Updates – Regular maintenance tasks, such as patching and updating network devices, can be automated. This ensures that the network remains secure and up-to-date with minimal manual intervention.

Network automation, with Ansible at its core, is redefining the way networks are managed and operated. It's a complex yet rewarding field that promises efficiency, reliability, and innovation. Whether it's managing a small local network or a vast cloud-based environment, Ansible's network automation capabilities provide the tools needed to succeed in this dynamic landscape.

Automated Configuration of Network Devices

Automated Configuration Process

Automating the configuration of network devices using Ansible involves a series of well-defined process steps. The process begins by defining the desired state of the switch in an Ansible playbook, which is a YAML file containing instructions for the automation.

Here, I'll walk you through the process with a practical example of configuring a Cisco switch.

1. First, we establish a connection to the Cisco device using Ansible's built-in networking modules, ensuring secure and reliable communication. The playbook then outlines the specific configurations required, such as VLAN settings, interface configurations, or access control lists. These configurations are defined in a clear, human-readable format, making it easy to understand and modify.
2. Next, Ansible's idempotent nature ensures that these configurations are applied only if necessary, preventing redundant changes and minimizing potential disruptions. The playbook is executed from the control node, which pushes the configurations to the Cisco switch. Ansible communicates over SSH, using either credentials or SSH keys for authentication.
3. Throughout the process, Ansible provides feedback and logging information, allowing for real-time monitoring and troubleshooting of the configuration process. This visibility is crucial for ensuring the accuracy and success of the automation.
4. Finally, Ansible allows for scalability and repeatability. The same playbook can be applied to multiple switches in the network, ensuring consistent configurations across the infrastructure.

Sample Program: Automate VLAN Configuration using Ansible

Now let us try to work around Cisco switch, wherein we want to automate the configuration of its VLAN (Virtual Local Area Network). Specifically, we'll create a new VLAN with ID 100, name it 'Guest_VLAN,' and assign a range of ports to it.

Following is a step-by-step walkthrough:

Inventory File
Create an inventory file named hosts.ini that defines the Cisco switch.

```
[switches]
cisco_switch ansible_host=192.168.1.1 ansible_user=admin ansible_password=secret
```

Create a Playbook
Create a playbook named configure_vlan.yaml to automate the VLAN configuration.

```
---
- hosts: switches
  gather_facts: no
  connection: network_cli

  tasks:
    - name: Create VLAN 100
      ios_vlan:
        vlan_id: 100
        name: Guest_VLAN
        state: present

    - name: Assign ports to VLAN 100
      ios_l2_interfaces:
        name: "{{ item }}"
        mode: access
        access_vlan: 100
      loop:
        - GigabitEthernet0/1
        - GigabitEthernet0/2
        - GigabitEthernet0/3
```

Here, the playbook uses two specific Ansible modules:

- ios_vlan: Manages VLAN configurations on IOS devices.
- ios_l2_interfaces: Manages Layer-2 interface configurations on IOS devices.

Running Playbook
Execute the playbook using the following command:

```
ansible-playbook -i hosts.ini configure_vlan.yaml
```

Verification
You can manually SSH into the Cisco switch and run the command show vlan to verify the configuration.

The above example showed how to use Ansible to automate the configuration of a Cisco switch by creating a new VLAN and assigning ports to it. The playbook makes use of Ansible modules designed specifically for interacting with Cisco IOS devices. The benefit of this method is that the same playbook can be used on multiple devices by simply updating the inventory file. You can extend this to include other configuration aspects by following similar patterns, allowing for efficient, consistent, and error-free network configuration.

Automate Complex VLAN & Multiple Switches

Let's extend our previous scenario by adding more complexity. In the below sample program, we'll automate the configuration of multiple switches and routers, incorporating VLANs, OSPF routing, and user access management using Ansible. This will provide a more comprehensive view of network automation.

Imagine a network containing multiple Cisco switches and routers. We want to configure VLANs across switches, set up OSPF (Open Shortest Path First) routing on the routers, and manage user access rights.

Following is a step-by-step walkthrough:

Inventory File
Create an inventory file named network_devices.ini, dividing the devices into routers and switches.

```
[switches]
switch1 ansible_host=192.168.1.1 ansible_user=admin ansible_password=secret
switch2 ansible_host=192.168.1.2 ansible_user=admin ansible_password=secret

[routers]
router1 ansible_host=192.168.1.3 ansible_user=admin ansible_password=secret
```

```
router2 ansible_host=192.168.1.4 ansible_user=admin ansible_password=secret
```

VLAN Configuration Playbook

Create a playbook named configure_vlan.yaml for VLAN setup.

```
---
- hosts: switches
  gather_facts: no
  connection: network_cli

  tasks:
    - name: Create VLAN 100
      ios_vlan:
        vlan_id: 100
        name: Guest_VLAN
        state: present
    - name: Assign ports to VLAN 100
      ios_l2_interfaces:
        name: "{{ item }}"
        mode: access
        access_vlan: 100
      loop:
        - GigabitEthernet0/1
        - GigabitEthernet0/2
```

OSPF Configuration Playbook

Create a playbook named configure_ospf.yaml for OSPF setup.

```
---
- hosts: routers
  gather_facts: no
  connection: network_cli
  tasks:
    - name: Configure OSPF
```

```
    ios_ospf:
      processes:
        - id: 1
          networks:
            - area: 0.0.0.0
              prefix: 192.168.0.0/16
```

User Management Playbook

Create a playbook named user_management.yaml to manage user access.

```
---
- hosts: switches:routers
  gather_facts: no
  connection: network_cli
  tasks:
    - name: Create User
      ios_user:
        name: user1
        password: user_password
        privilege: 15
        state: present
```

Running the Playbooks

Execute each playbook separately using the following commands:

```
ansible-playbook -i network_devices.ini configure_vlan.yaml
ansible-playbook -i network_devices.ini configure_ospf.yaml
ansible-playbook -i network_devices.ini user_management.yaml
```

Verification

SSH into the devices to verify the configurations.

Overall, we've demonstrated a multifaceted configuration involving VLANs, OSPF routing, and user management. The above example showcases the power of Ansible in orchestrating complex network scenarios and illustrates how various network automation tasks can be interlinked.

Automate Software Upgrades

Automating software upgrades is an essential aspect of network management. Performing these upgrades manually across a large number of devices can be time-consuming and error-prone. Using Ansible, you can streamline this process, ensuring that all devices are running the required software versions.

In the below sample program, we'll look at how to automate the software upgrade process on Cisco network devices, such as routers and switches. Let us consider that have a network consisting of multiple Cisco switches and routers as considered in the previous examples. And, now you want to automate the software upgrade process across these devices to a specific IOS (Internetwork Operating System) version.

Following is a step-by-step walkthrough:

Inventory File

Start by defining an inventory file named network_devices.ini with all the devices.

```
[network_devices]
device1 ansible_host=192.168.1.1 ansible_user=admin ansible_password=secret
device2 ansible_host=192.168.1.2 ansible_user=admin ansible_password=secret
```

Create Directory for Images

Locally, create a directory to store the IOS images for the upgrade.

```
mkdir ios_images
```

Place the necessary IOS images in this directory.

File Transfer Playbook

First, we'll create a playbook to transfer the IOS images to the devices. We shall call it transfer_ios.yaml.

```
---
- hosts: network_devices
  gather_facts: no
  connection: network_cli
  tasks:
```

```
  - name: Transfer IOS Image to Device
    ansible.builtin.copy:
      src: "ios_images/{{ ios_image_file }}"
      dest: "flash:/{{ ios_image_file }}"
```

You'll need to set the variable ios_image_file to the name of the IOS image for each device.

Upgrade Playbook

Next, create a playbook to initiate the upgrade, named upgrade_ios.yaml.

```
---
- hosts: network_devices
  gather_facts: no
  connection: network_cli
  tasks:
    - name: Set Boot System
      ios_command:
        commands:
          - command: "boot system flash:/{{ ios_image_file }}"
          - command: "write memory"
    - name: Reload Device
      ios_command:
        commands:
          - command: "reload"
        prompt:
          - "[confirm]"
        answer:
          - ""
```

This playbook configures the boot system to use the new IOS image and then reloads the device.

Running the Playbooks

Execute the playbooks sequentially with the appropriate inventory file and variable.

ansible-playbook -i network_devices.ini transfer_ios.yaml --extra-vars

```
"ios_image_file=your_ios_image.bin"
ansible-playbook -i network_devices.ini upgrade_ios.yaml --extra-vars "ios_image_file=your_ios_image.bin"
```

Verification

SSH into the devices to verify the IOS version using the show version command. The playbooks created transfer the necessary IOS images to the devices, configure them to boot from these images, and then reload the devices to apply the upgrades.

The above example demonstrates the power of Ansible in handling even the more advanced aspects of network management, enabling administrators to maintain a consistent environment across their entire network. The same principles can be adapted to different network vendors and devices, making Ansible a versatile tool in network automation.

Errors & Troubleshooting

Network management often involves dealing with recurring and common errors that might disrupt the smooth functioning of the system. Network administrators can automate the detection and remediation of these common issues using right set of Ansible commands, tools and strategies.

Below, we will explore some of the popular and commonly occurred network errors and demonstrate how Ansible can be used to address them.

Error#1: Port Security Violation

A common error occurs when there's a port security violation on a switch, preventing legitimate devices from connecting to the network.

To address this error, we'll create an Ansible playbook to monitor and reset the port security violation.

Sample Playbook for Monitoring Port Security Violation

```
---
- hosts: switches
  gather_facts: no
  connection: network_cli
  tasks
    - name: Check Port Security Violation
```

```
    ios_command:
      commands:
        - command: "show port-security interface GigabitEthernet0/1"
    register: result

  - name: Alert on Violation
    debug:
      msg: "Port Security Violation detected on GigabitEthernet0/1"
    when: "'Violation Mode' in result.stdout[0]"
```

Sample Playbook for Resetting the Violation

```
---
- hosts: switches
  gather_facts: no
  connection: network_cli
  tasks
  - name: Reset Port Security Violation
    ios_command:
      commands:
        - command: "clear port-security sticky interface GigabitEthernet0/1"
```

These playbooks can be scheduled to run periodically to monitor and automatically reset port security violations.

Error#2: Duplicate IP Address

Another common network error is a duplicate IP address conflict, where two devices are assigned the same IP address.

To address this issue, let us create an Ansible playbook to detect duplicate IP addresses and send an alert.

Sample Playbook for Detecting Duplicate IP Addresses

```
---
```

```
- hosts: routers
  gather_facts: no
  connection: network_cli

  tasks
    - name: Check IP Conflict
      ios_command:
        commands:
          - command: "show ip dhcp conflict"
      register: conflict

    - name: Alert on IP Conflict
      debug:
        msg: "Duplicate IP Address detected"
      when: conflict.stdout[0] != ''
```

This playbook will detect any duplicate IP addresses in the DHCP conflicts and send an alert, allowing network administrators to investigate and resolve the conflict manually.

Error#3: High Bandwidth Utilization

Bandwidth overutilization on specific links might slow down the entire network, causing significant delays in data transmission.

To address this bandwidth issue, you can use Ansible to monitor bandwidth utilization and balance the load by redirecting traffic if the utilization crosses a particular threshold.

Sample Playbook for Monitoring and Redirecting Bandwidth

```
---
- hosts: routers
  gather_facts: no
  connection: network_cli

  tasks
    - name: Check Bandwidth Utilization
```

```
    ios_command:
      commands:
        - command: "show interfaces | include GigabitEthernet0/1"
    register: bandwidth

  - name: Redirect Traffic
    ios_config:
      lines:
        - command: "ip route x.x.x.x y.y.y.y z.z.z.z"
    when: "'800 Mbps' in bandwidth.stdout[0]"
```

This playbook will detect the bandwidth utilization on the specific interface and add a new routing entry to balance the load if the utilization crosses 800 Mbps.

Error#4: Inactive Network Devices

Inactive or down network devices can lead to network disruption and impact the availability of services.

To address such issue, let us create an Ansible playbook to monitor the status of network devices and restart them if they are down.

Sample Playbook for Monitoring and Restarting Network Devices

```
---
- hosts: all_devices
  gather_facts: no
  connection: network_cli

  tasks
  - name: Check Device Status
    ios_command:
      commands:
        - command: "show ip interface brief"
    register: status
```

```
- name: Restart Device
  ios_command:
    commands:
      - command: "reload"
  when: "'down' in status.stdout[0]"
```

This playbook will monitor the status of network devices, and if any device is found to be down, it will reload it.

Through continuous monitoring and automation, network administrators can ensure optimal performance and rapid response to emerging issues. Ansible's ability to automate these complex and repetitive tasks not only enhances the efficiency and reliability of the network but also frees up valuable time and resources for other strategic initiatives.

Summary

In this chapter, the primary focus was on gaining an understanding of network automation and the significant role that Ansible plays in this field. The first part of the chapter provided an introduction to the idea of network automation, including an explanation of its advantages and the role that Ansible plays in automating a variety of network tasks. It was emphasized that Ansible is flexible and efficient in managing complex network environments, demonstrating its adaptability to a variety of network architectures and specific business requirements.

The chapter guided you through the process of automating tasks such as configuring network devices, performing software upgrades, and addressing common network errors by providing them with practical examples and demonstrations. The automation of complex network scenarios, such as high bandwidth utilization and the management of inactive network devices, was the purpose of these examples, which were provided for educational purposes. This chapter provided valuable information about the utilization of Ansible for the purpose of monitoring, controlling, and streamlining network operations. As a result, the chapter contributed to the enhancement of the effectiveness and dependability of network systems.

Lastly, the chapter offered a comprehensive analysis of how Ansible can be utilized to address issues that occur in the real world and guarantee the best possible performance of a network. You gained an understanding of how to make use of the powerful features that Ansible offers in order to keep the network in good health and stability by creating playbooks that were specifically tailored to specific issues such as bandwidth monitoring, traffic redirection, and device restarting. The practical examples demonstrated the power of Ansible to transform manual processes that are prone to errors into automated solutions that are repeatable and scalable. As a result, Ansible has become an indispensable tool in the practice of modern network management.

CHAPTER 7: ANSIBLE FOR DEVOPS

Understand DevOps in Ansible

Understanding DevOps in the context of Ansible involves recognizing the significant shift that this methodology brings to the realm of software development and IT operations. DevOps is more than just a set of practices or tools; it represents a fundamental change in the culture and approach to the entire software delivery lifecycle.

DevOps merges the traditionally siloed roles of software development (Dev) and IT operations (Ops), fostering a culture of collaboration and shared responsibility. The goal is to bridge the gap between these two departments, ensuring that software is not only developed but also deployed and maintained in the most efficient, automated, and error-free manner possible.

A core tenet of DevOps is CI/CD. Continuous Integration (CI) involves the practice of frequently merging code changes into a central repository, where automated builds and tests are run. Continuous Delivery (CD) extends this concept by ensuring that the software can be released to production at any time. These practices enable teams to detect problems early, deliver updates faster, and make the release process more predictable and less risky.

DevOps emphasizes rapid iteration - the ability to quickly develop, test, and release software. This rapidity is achieved through automated pipelines that provide instant feedback on the changes made. These feedback loops are crucial for continuous improvement and play a significant role in maintaining high software quality.

Principle behind DevOps

DevOps, as a transformative approach to software development and IT operations, is anchored in several core principles that collectively aim to enhance the efficiency, quality, and agility of the software delivery process. These principles not only guide practices and tool choices but also shape the underlying culture and mindset of the teams involved.

Automation

In the DevOps world, automation stands as the cornerstone principle. It involves replacing manual, repetitive, and error-prone operations with automated processes using code, scripts, and specialized tools. This shift is crucial for several reasons:

- Efficiency and Speed: Automation significantly speeds up various stages of the software development lifecycle, from code integration to deployment and infrastructure provisioning. It allows teams to deliver software faster and more reliably.
- Consistency and Reliability: Automated processes are consistent and repeatable, reducing the likelihood of errors that are common in manual processes. This consistency ensures a more stable and reliable IT environment.

- Scaling Operations: Automation makes it easier to scale operations. As the infrastructure or the application grows, automated processes can be scaled up to accommodate this growth without a proportional increase in effort or complexity.

Collaboration

Collaboration is another pillar of DevOps. This principle emphasizes the breaking down of silos between development and operations teams, fostering a culture of open communication and cooperation. Effective collaboration leads to:

- Shared Responsibility: Encouraging a sense of shared responsibility for the software's performance and health fosters a more cooperative and productive working environment.
- Cross-functional Teams: By having teams with cross-functional skills, organizations can ensure smooth transitions of software from development to production.
- Faster Problem-Solving: Better collaboration leads to faster identification and resolution of issues, enhancing the overall quality of the software.

Continuous Integration and Continuous Deployment

CI/CD is the heartbeat of the DevOps methodology:

- Continuous Integration: CI involves developers frequently merging their code changes into a central repository, where automated builds and tests are run. This practice helps in identifying and addressing bugs early, improving software quality.
- Continuous Deployment: CD takes the process further by ensuring that every change that passes the automated tests can be automatically deployed to production. This continuous flow creates a rapid feedback loop and accelerates the release cycle.

Measurement and Monitoring

In DevOps, data-driven decision-making is key. Measurement and monitoring involve:

- Performance Metrics: Tracking key performance indicators (KPIs) of applications and infrastructure to ensure they meet performance goals.
- User Experience: Monitoring user experience metrics to ensure that the software meets customer needs and expectations.
- Feedback Loops: Using monitoring data to create feedback loops that inform development and operational decisions, leading to continuous improvement.

Lean Process Improvement

DevOps embraces lean principles, focusing on creating more value for customers with fewer resources:

- Eliminating Waste: Identifying and eliminating activities that do not add value to the software development process.
- Optimizing Processes: Continuously analyzing and improving processes to enhance efficiency and effectiveness.
- Value Stream Mapping: Understanding the flow of value through the development process and optimizing it for maximum efficiency and minimum waste.

To summarize, Ansible's alignment with the DevOps philosophy brings agility, efficiency, and synergy to the software development process. Its emphasis on automation, collaboration, and integration makes it a crucial tool in modern DevOps practices, transforming the way software is developed, deployed, and maintained.

Continuous Integration and Continuous Deployment Pipelines

Continuous Integration/Continuous Deployment (CI/CD) is a core aspect of the modern DevOps practice. CI/CD pipelines provide an automated way to build, test, and deploy code, ensuring a consistent and efficient software development lifecycle. Let's delve into the architecture and components of CI/CD pipelines.

Continuous Integration (CI)

Continuous Integration (CI) involves the ongoing merging or integrating of code changes from different contributors. As developers commit changes to a shared repository, the CI system builds, tests, and validates the code, ensuring that it integrates seamlessly with existing code.

Key Components of CI

- Source Code Repository: A centralized place where the code is stored, such as Git.
- Build Automation: Automatically compiles and builds the code into executable artifacts.
- Automated Testing: Executes various types of tests (unit, integration, etc.) to validate the code.
- Integration Server: A server like Jenkins that orchestrates the entire CI process.
- Notification System: Alerts developers about build status, failures, or successes.

Continuous Deployment (CD)

Continuous Deployment (CD) is an extension of CI that automates the deployment of code to different environments, from development and staging to production. This ensures that the code is always in a deployable state.

Key Components of CD

- Environment Provisioning: Automatically sets up the required infrastructure for deployment.
- Deployment Automation: Automatically deploys the build artifacts to different environments.
- Monitoring and Logging: Constantly monitors the application and collects logs for analysis.
- Rollback Mechanisms: Allows for quick rollback in case of failures.

CI/CD Pipeline Architecture

The CI/CD (Continuous Integration/Continuous Deployment) pipeline represents the backbone of modern DevOps practices, establishing a streamlined pathway for taking software from development to deployment. This pipeline embodies a series of stages, each with specific tasks and objectives, working together to ensure that software is delivered efficiently, reliably, and with high quality. Let's expand upon the typical architecture of a CI/CD pipeline:

Development Phase

- Code Commitment: This initial stage involves developers writing and committing code to a shared version control repository, such as Git. Committing code frequently encourages smaller, more manageable changes and faster integration cycles.
- Code Review: After committing code, peer reviews are conducted to ensure quality and adherence to coding standards. Code reviews are crucial for maintaining code quality, sharing knowledge among team members, and catching potential issues early in the development process.
- Branching Strategy: Implementing a robust branching strategy (like Gitflow) ensures organized development and feature integration, allowing multiple developers to work on different features simultaneously without disrupting the main codebase.

Integration Phase (CI)

- Automated Build: The CI server automatically compiles the code into binary artifacts upon new commits in the repository. This stage may also include packaging the application for deployment.
- Automated Testing: Automated tests are run to ensure the new code doesn't break existing functionality. This includes unit tests, integration tests, and acceptance tests, which validate different aspects of the software.
- Code Analysis: Automated code quality and security tools analyze the source code for potential issues like coding standard violations, security vulnerabilities, or technical debt. This step is critical for maintaining high code quality and security standards.
- Artifact Repository: Successful builds are stored in an artifact repository, creating a central hub for all deployable artifacts and ensuring version control of the build outputs.

Deployment Phase (CD)

- Staging Deployment: Before deployment to production, the application is deployed to a staging environment. This environment mirrors the production setting and is used for final testing and validation to ensure that the application behaves as expected in a production-like setting.
- Approval and Rollout Strategy: Depending on the organization's policy, there might be an approval process before the final deployment. Additionally, deployment strategies like blue-green deployments or canary releases can be employed for safer rollouts.
- Production Deployment: The final deployment to the production environment is where the application becomes available to end-users. This step can be automated to allow seamless and rapid deployment of new features and fixes.
- Monitoring and Performance Tracking: Continuous monitoring of the application in production is crucial. This involves tracking performance metrics, user behavior, and system health to ensure the application performs reliably and efficiently under real-world conditions.
- Feedback Loop: The insights gained from monitoring feed back into the development process, informing developers of issues, user experience, and performance in the real world. This feedback loop is vital for continuous improvement of the application.

Post-Deployment

- Post-Deployment Testing: Even after deployment, tests can be run to ensure that the application performs as expected in the production environment.

- Incident Response: Quick response to any issues or incidents in the production environment is crucial. Automating certain responses, like rolling back to a previous version, can be part of the CD process.
- Continuous Learning and Improvement: The CI/CD pipeline is a living process. Teams should regularly review and refine their CI/CD practices based on lessons learned, evolving technologies, and changing business requirements.

By encapsulating the principles of automation, collaboration, and continuous improvement, continuous integration and continuous delivery pipelines are an essential component of contemporary software development practices. By integrating with Ansible, continuous integration and continuous delivery pipelines become more powerful and flexible, which in turn improves the ability to deliver high-quality software at a faster rate.

Integrate Ansible Playbooks with Jenkins

Integrating Ansible with Jenkins offers a seamless way to automate various stages of the Continuous Integration and Continuous Deployment (CI/CD) pipeline. This includes tasks like environment provisioning, code deployment, configuration management, and more. Following is a practical demonstration of how to integrate Ansible playbooks with Jenkins.

Setting up Jenkins

Install Necessary Plugins

- Go to "Manage Jenkins" > "Manage Plugins."
- Install the "Ansible plugin" from the available list.
- Restart Jenkins if required.

Configure Ansible in Jenkins

- Navigate to "Manage Jenkins" > "Global Tool Configuration."
- Scroll down to the Ansible section and click "Add Ansible."
- Provide a name for the configuration and the path to the Ansible installation.
- Save the configuration.

Creating Jenkins Job

Create New Job

- Go to the Jenkins dashboard and click on "New Item."

- Enter a name for the job, select "Freestyle project," and click "OK."

Configure Source Code Management

- In the job configuration, navigate to the "Source Code Management" section.
- Choose the source code repository type (e.g., Git) and provide the repository URL.
- Specify the branch if necessary.

Add Ansible Playbook Build Step

- Scroll down to the "Build" section and click "Add build step" > "Invoke Ansible Playbook."
- Select the Ansible installation configured earlier.
- Provide the path to the playbook file or the inline content of the playbook.
- Specify additional parameters like inventory file, credentials, extra variables, etc., if required.

Configure Post-Build Actions

- You may add post-build actions such as sending notifications, archiving artifacts, etc., based on your needs.

Save and Run the Job

- Click "Save" to save the job configuration.
- Click "Build Now" to run the job.

Following is a simple example of an Ansible playbook that you might use to deploy a web server:

```
---
- hosts: web_servers
  tasks:
    - name: Install Apache
      yum:
        name: httpd
        state: present
```

```
- name: Start Apache
  service:
    name: httpd
    state: started
```

This playbook can be part of the Jenkins job, and upon running the job, Ansible will execute this playbook on the target hosts defined in the inventory file.

Monitoring and Logging

- Jenkins provides detailed build logs, allowing you to track the progress of the Ansible playbook execution.
- You can also integrate additional tools for monitoring and logging to gain insights into the deployment process.

Advanced Integrations

- You may integrate additional tools and plugins to extend the capabilities, such as integrating with Docker, Kubernetes, or other CI/CD tools.
- Utilizing Ansible roles and modules can further optimize and modularize the automation process.

By integrating Ansible and Jenkins in a continuous integration and continuous delivery pipeline, you will be able to automate difficult tasks, which will reduce the amount of time spent on the development and deployment process overall. You will be led through the necessary steps to configure Jenkins and Ansible, as well as to define a job and execute an Ansible playbook, by attending this demonstration. The specific requirements of the project and the infrastructure requirements can be used to guide the exploration of advanced integrations and customizations.

Integrate Ansible Playbooks with Docker

The integration of Ansible and Docker results in a powerful combination that can be used to automate certain containerization tasks. Ansible provides modules that make it simple to manage Docker containers, images, networks, and volumes. A number of these modules are available. To demonstrate how you can use Ansible to work with Docker, the following practical walkthrough provides a comprehensive demonstration.

Ansible Docker Modules

Ansible offers several modules to interact with Docker:

- docker_container: Manages Docker containers.
- docker_image: Manages Docker images.
- docker_network: Manages Docker networks.
- docker_volume: Manages Docker volumes.

Sample Playbooks

Here, we'll outline some practical examples demonstrating different Docker-related tasks using Ansible.

Pulling a Docker Image

```
---
- name: Pull NGINX image
  hosts: target
  tasks:
    - name: Ensure NGINX image is present
      docker_image:
        name: nginx
        source: pull
```

Creating Docker Container

```
---
- name: Run NGINX container
  hosts: target
  tasks:
    - name: Ensure NGINX container is running
      docker_container:
        name: webserver
        image: nginx
        state: started
        ports:
          - "8080:80"
```

Managing Docker Networks

```
---
- name: Manage Docker Network
  hosts: target
  tasks:
    - name: Create custom network
      docker_network:
        name: custom_network
        state: present

    - name: Add NGINX container to custom network
      docker_container:
        name: webserver
        networks:
          - name: custom_network
```

Managing Docker Volumes

```
---
- name: Manage Docker Volume
  hosts: target
  tasks:
    - name: Create custom volume
      docker_volume:
        name: custom_volume
        state: present

    - name: Add custom volume to NGINX container
      docker_container:
        name: webserver
        volumes:
          - custom_volume:/usr/share/nginx/html
```

Running Playbooks

To run these playbooks, use the following command:

```
ansible-playbook -i inventory.ini playbook.yml
```

Make sure that the target machine has the necessary Docker permissions and dependencies.

Docker and Ansible Roles Integration

You can create Ansible roles to encapsulate specific Docker-related functionalities, such as setting up a specific service, managing networks, or handling volumes. By modularizing these tasks into roles, you enhance reusability and maintainability.

You may further integrate Ansible with tools like Docker Compose or Kubernetes for more advanced container orchestration capabilities. From image handling to complex network configurations, Ansible provides modules that simplify these tasks. By following this demonstration and applying best practices, you can develop sophisticated automation solutions for your Docker environments.

Integrate Ansible Playbooks with Kubernetes

Integrating Ansible with Kubernetes opens up opportunities to manage container orchestration in a more automated and efficient way. Ansible offers the ability to create and manage Kubernetes resources with ease through its modules and dynamic inventory plugins. This practical demonstration will guide you through the process of integrating Ansible with Kubernetes to handle tasks such as deploying applications, managing configurations, and scaling resources.

Ansible Kubernetes Modules

Ansible offers various modules to interact with Kubernetes resources, including:

- k8s: General-purpose module to manage Kubernetes resources.
- k8s_info: Retrieves information about Kubernetes resources.

Kubernetes Inventory Plugin

Ansible also provides an inventory plugin to dynamically retrieve information about Kubernetes resources, enabling you to target specific nodes, pods, or other resources.

Sample Playbook

Deploying an Application

```
---
- name: Deploy NGINX application on Kubernetes
  hosts: localhost
  tasks:
    - name: Create deployment
      k8s:
        kubeconfig: /path/to/kubeconfig
        state: present
        definition:
          apiVersion: apps/v1
          kind: Deployment
          metadata:
            name: nginx-deployment
            namespace: default
          spec:
            replicas: 2
            selector:
              matchLabels:
                app: nginx
            template:
              metadata:
                labels:
                  app: nginx
              spec:
                containers:
                  - name: nginx
                    image: nginx:1.16
                    ports:
                      - containerPort: 80
```

Managing Configurations (ConfigMap)

```
---
```

```
- name: Manage ConfigMap
  hosts: localhost
  tasks:
    - name: Create ConfigMap
      k8s:
        kubeconfig: /path/to/kubeconfig
        state: present
        definition:
          apiVersion: v1
          kind: ConfigMap
          metadata:
            name: app-config
            namespace: default
          data:
            app.properties: |
              key=value
```

Scaling Resources (Horizontal Pod Autoscaler)

```
---
- name: Create Horizontal Pod Autoscaler
  hosts: localhost
  tasks:
    - name: Apply HPA
      k8s:
        kubeconfig: /path/to/kubeconfig
        state: present
        definition:
          apiVersion: autoscaling/v2beta2
          kind: HorizontalPodAutoscaler
          metadata:
            name: nginx-hpa
            namespace: default
```

```
spec:
  scaleTargetRef:
    apiVersion: apps/v1
    kind: Deployment
    name: nginx-deployment
  minReplicas: 1
  maxReplicas: 10
  metrics:
    - type: Resource
      resource:
        name: cpu
        target:
          type: Utilization
          averageUtilization: 50
```

Running Playbooks

Execute the playbooks using the following command:

```
ansible-playbook -i /path/to/inventory.ini playbook.yml
```

The combination of Kubernetes and Ansible creates a potent set of tools for the management of container orchestration tasks. With the help of Ansible modules, deploying, scaling, and configuring applications inside of Kubernetes is a breeze. Although this demonstration serves as a starting point, the potential applications are extremely diverse and can range from straightforward deployments to intricate multi-tier applications.

Summary

In this chapter, we looked at how to integrate Ansible with DevOps tools like Jenkins, Docker, and Kubernetes. We started by learning about the fundamentals of DevOps and how Ansible contributes to CI/CD pipelines by promoting automation and collaboration between development and operations teams.

We integrated Ansible with Jenkins through practical demonstrations, demonstrating how Ansible playbooks can be triggered within Jenkins pipelines to automate deployment processes. We also looked into integrating Ansible and Docker to demonstrate the automation of container management tasks like building, deploying, and scaling Docker containers. This allowed us to see how Ansible adds a layer of automation to container orchestration, making complex containerized applications easier to manage.

This chapter was dominated by the integration of Ansible and Kubernetes. We created and managed Kubernetes resources by understanding the available Ansible modules for Kubernetes and the dynamic inventory plugin. Ansible playbooks were used to deploy applications, manage configurations, and scale resources within Kubernetes. We also learned Role-Based Access Control (RBAC), version compatibility, idempotency, and error handling. Overall, this chapter provided in-depth insights into Ansible's flexibility and power within the DevOps ecosystem, highlighting its role in automating complex deployment and management tasks across multiple platforms.

CHAPTER 8: TROUBLESHOOTING ANSIBLE

Introduction to Debugging in Ansible

The process of debugging, which is an essential part of the software development and automation industries, is an essential component of Ansible's ecosystem. In the complex dance that is automation, in which every step, from the execution of the playbook to the interaction of the modules, needs to be painstakingly choreographed, debugging guarantees that the performance will be flawless. It is the sharp eye that can spot mistakes, the steady hand that can correct them, and the astute mind that can stop them from happening in the first place.

When working with Ansible, debugging takes on a number of different dimensions, each of which corresponds to a different facet of automation, including networking, performance, and security and various techniques of debugging forms a paramount to make the best use of Ansible at work.

Network Errors

Connection Errors

- Connection errors in Ansible are akin to trying to start a conversation but finding the phone line dead. They surface when Ansible cannot establish a connection with a host, often rooted in SSH key mismatches, firewall configurations acting as unyielding gatekeepers, network settings leading to wrong turns, or simply, the host being unavailable - a door to a critical resource firmly shut.
- Debugging involves checking the integrity of SSH keys, ensuring firewalls are configured to allow necessary traffic, validating network configurations, and confirming host availability.

Timeout Errors

- When a network conversation drags on too long and Ansible's patience wears thin, timeout errors occur. They are the result of prolonged connection attempts or commands that overstay their welcome, often caused by network latency acting as an unwanted pause, timeout settings miscalibrated, or tasks that are too demanding.
- To mitigate these, one must scrutinize the network paths for bottlenecks, adjust timeout settings to accommodate expected delays, and break down or optimize lengthy tasks.

Authentication Failures

- These errors emerge when Ansible's identity is questioned, and credentials are found wanting. Incorrect login credentials or insufficient permissions are the usual culprits.
- The resolution path involves ensuring that the provided credentials are correct and that the user account has the necessary permissions for the intended tasks.

Performance Errors

Resource Constraints

- When Ansible's playbooks try to perform their act but find the stage too small, resource constraints come into play. Limited CPU, memory, or disk space are the typical constraints that can turn a smooth performance into a stuttering ordeal.
- Addressing this involves optimizing resource usage, upgrading hardware where feasible, or splitting tasks across multiple systems.

Parallelism and Throttling

- The art of parallelism in Ansible is like conducting an orchestra; too many instruments playing at once can overwhelm. Inadequately managed parallel execution or overloading hosts can lead to a cacophony, harming overall performance.
- Fine-tuning the level of parallelism and using throttling settings judiciously can ensure a harmonious performance.

Inefficient Playbooks

- An inefficient playbook is like a script laden with unnecessary dialogues and scenes. Tasks that serve little purpose, repeated calls that echo without need, or unoptimized code are the usual suspects.
- Refactoring playbooks, removing redundant tasks, and optimizing code can transform a cumbersome script into a streamlined narrative.

Security Errors

Permission Issues

- Overstepping or underutilizing permissions in Ansible is like walking a tightrope; too much or too little can lead to a fall. Excessive permissions can expose vulnerabilities, while insufficient permissions can halt tasks mid-stride.
- The key is to balance permissions - granting enough to perform tasks effectively but not so much that it opens doors to potential threats.

Insecure Content

- Using insecure content or communication channels is akin to sending secret messages through a public loudspeaker. It risks the integrity and confidentiality of the automated system.

- Ensuring encryption in data transfer and avoiding the use of unsecured content can uphold the sanctity of the system.

Compliance Failures

- Automation that doesn't align with compliance standards is like a play ignoring its regulatory script. It can lead to security breaches and legal repercussions.
- Ensuring that all automation tasks comply with organizational and regulatory standards is crucial.

Debugging Techniques

Verbose Logging

- Verbose logging in Ansible is like turning on brighter stage lights to see every actor's move. It sheds light on the inner workings of playbooks, revealing where and why they stumble.
- Utilizing various verbosity levels, one can gain insights into each step of the playbook execution.

Debug Module

- The debug module is Ansible's magnifying glass, allowing you to examine variables and states at various points.
- It's instrumental in dissecting complex playbooks to understand their behavior at specific junctures.

Error Handling

- Ansible's error handling is its safety net, catching tasks before they fall. Utilizing features like ignore_errors, failed_when, and rescue blocks allows for graceful handling of unexpected situations.
- This level of control is crucial in maintaining the stability and reliability of automation processes.

Callback Plugins

- Callback plugins in Ansible are the directors behind the scenes, shaping the output of playbook executions. They customize how results are displayed and logged.
- This customization can be pivotal in aligning the output with monitoring systems or specific logging requirements.

In order to keep the reliability, efficiency, and security of the automation tasks that are implemented through Ansible, it is essential to gain an understanding of the various errors that can occur and the underlying causes of those errors, in addition to employing the appropriate debugging techniques.

Ansible Debugging Techniques

Debugging techniques in Ansible are essential for identifying and resolving issues within playbooks, modules, and other components of automation. Various methods and tools can be leveraged to help with this process, each serving a specific purpose and providing different insights.

Verbose Logging

Functionality

- -v: Basic verbosity, provides a high-level overview.
- -vv: More detailed, includes information about the invocation.
- -vvv: Even more detailed, shows the exact command being executed.
- -vvvv: Maximum verbosity, provides complete information, including connection details.

Usage

The verbosity level can be set when running a playbook using the ansible-playbook command. For example, ansible-playbook -vv playbook.yml.

Benefit

Helps in identifying where the playbook might be failing or performing poorly.

Debug Module

Functionality

Allows you to print custom messages and variable values at different stages of playbook execution.

Usage

```
- debug:
    msg: "The value of variable_a is {{ variable_a }}"
```

Benefit

Great for examining the values of variables during playbook execution, making it easier to find logical errors.

Error Handling

Ignore Errors

Continues playbook execution even if a task fails.

```
- name: This will not stop the playbook
  command: /bin/false
  ignore_errors: yes
```

Failed When

Allows defining custom failure conditions.

```
- name: Fail task when variable is 0
  command: /bin/something
  register: result
  failed_when: result.rc == 0
```

Blocks, Rescue, and Always

Helps in grouping tasks and handling errors.

```
block:
- name: This might fail
  command: /bin/something

rescue:
- name: This will be executed if block fails
  debug:
    msg: "Error found"

always:
- name: This will always execute
  debug:
```

```
msg: "Cleanup"
```

Benefit
Provides better control over how errors are handled, allowing graceful failure or custom responses to specific error conditions.

Using Callback Plugins

Functionality
Allows customization of the output from playbook execution.

Usage
Requires writing custom Python code and configuring Ansible to use the new callback plugin.

Benefit
Can be used to integrate with external logging or monitoring systems or to provide custom output formats.

Profiling Tasks

Functionality
Helps in identifying slow-running tasks within a playbook.

Usage
Ansible provides a profile_tasks callback plugin that can be enabled in the configuration file.

Benefit
Identifies performance bottlenecks, which can be optimized to improve overall efficiency.

Static Code Analysis

ansible-lint
Helps in identifying syntax errors, stylistic issues, and violations of best practices.

Usage
Can be integrated into the development workflow or run manually against playbooks.

Benefit
Ensures adherence to coding standards, which improves maintainability and reduces the likelihood of errors.

Ad-hoc Commands

Functionality

Allows running individual commands without a playbook for quick testing.

Usage

Executing commands like ansible all -m ping for quick testing.

Benefit

Useful for rapid experimentation and verification of basic connectivity or functionality.

The purpose of debugging techniques in Ansible extends beyond simply correcting errors. They make an overall positive contribution to the quality, efficiency, and maintainability of automation projects. It is possible for developers and system administrators to construct automation with Ansible that is more robust, performant, and secure if they understand and effectively use these techniques. Utilizing these best practices in the appropriate combination can result in more resilient deployments and development cycles that run more smoothly.

Troubleshoot Ansible Errors

This section dives into a variety of typical errors encountered in Ansible, such as undefined variables, SSH connection issues, playbook syntax errors, task failures, permission problems, and more. Each error is meticulously described to provide clarity on how they manifest and impact Ansible playbooks. Following the description, practical solutions are demonstrated to efficiently resolve these issues along with examples, wherever possible. This approach not only aids in immediate troubleshooting but also helps in developing a proactive mindset to anticipate and prevent potential errors in future automation tasks, thereby enhancing the overall robustness and reliability of Ansible

Undefined Variable Error

Error Description

This error occurs when Ansible attempts to use a variable in a playbook that has not been defined anywhere. This often happens due to typos in variable names, omitting variable definitions, or when variables are not passed correctly between plays and roles.

Solution

To solve this issue, you can either define the variable in your playbook, role, or inventory file, or you can provide a default value using the default Jinja2 filter. This ensures that if the variable isn't defined elsewhere, a default value is used to prevent the task from failing.

Example:

```
- name: Print undefined variable with default value
  debug:
    msg: "{{ my_variable | default('Default Value') }}"
```

SSH Connection Error

Error Description

Occurs when Ansible fails to establish an SSH connection to a managed node. This can be due to various reasons such as incorrect SSH keys, incorrect hostname, user authentication issues, or network problems.

Solution

Verify the SSH configuration including the host, username, and SSH key file. Ensure the SSH keys are correctly set up on both the control node and the managed node. If using a custom SSH port or specific SSH options, these should also be correctly configured.

Example:

```
- hosts: target_host
  remote_user: remote_user
  vars:
    ansible_ssh_private_key_file: /path/to/private_key
  tasks:
    - name: Execute a command
      command: echo "Hello, World!"
```

Syntax Error in Playbook

Error Description

This error is encountered when there is a mistake in the YAML syntax of the playbook. Common issues include incorrect indentation, missing colons, or improper alignment of YAML dictionaries and lists.

Solution

Carefully review the playbook's syntax. Tools like yamllint can be useful for identifying and correcting syntax errors. Pay special attention to indentation levels and the format of lists and dictionaries.

Task Failed Error

Error Description

This error appears when a task in a playbook fails to execute as expected. This could be due to a variety of reasons, like incorrect commands, missing dependencies, or logical errors in the playbook.

Solution

Review the task for any apparent mistakes. Consider using Ansible's error handling options like ignore_errors or failed_when to manage expected failures. Ensure all dependencies for the task are met.

Example:

```
- name: Attempt to execute a command
  command: /path/to/command
  ignore_errors: yes
```

Missing Required Package

Error Description

This occurs when a task in a playbook requires a specific software package that is not installed on the target system.

Solution

Use Ansible's package management modules like apt or yum to install the required packages before executing the task.

Example:

```
- name: Ensure Python is installed
  apt:
    name: python3
    state: present
```

Incompatible Ansible Version

Error Description

Occurs when trying to use features or modules that are not supported in the version of Ansible being used.

Solution

Update Ansible to the latest version or modify the playbook to be compatible with the installed version. Review the Ansible documentation for version-specific features and modules.

Role Not Found

Error Description

This error happens when Ansible cannot find a specified role, either because it doesn't exist, or the path is incorrect.

Solution

Ensure that the role exists in the appropriate directory. If the role is not locally available, it can be installed using ansible-galaxy.

Example:

```
ansible-galaxy install username.rolename
```

Permission Denied

Error Description

This error occurs when Ansible attempts to perform a task on the target machine without having the necessary permissions.

Solution

Use the become directive in your playbook to gain elevated privileges. Ensure that the user Ansible connects with has the required sudo permissions.

Example:

```
- name: Task requiring elevated privileges
  become: yes
  command: some_privileged_command
```

Deprecation Warnings

Error Description

Warnings about using deprecated features in Ansible. These features are likely to be removed in future versions.

Solution
Update the playbook to use current methods and features as recommended in the latest Ansible documentation.

Invalid Inventory

Error Description
This error occurs when the inventory file is incorrectly formatted, hosts are unreachable, or the grouping is wrong.

Solution
Review the inventory file for correct syntax and grouping. Verify that all hosts are reachable and correctly defined.

Example:

```
[webservers]
webserver1.example.com
webserver2.example.com
```

Playbook Path Errors

Error Description
This error surfaces when Ansible cannot locate the specified playbook. This might occur if the playbook file is misplaced, incorrectly named, or if there's a typo in the file path.

Solution
Check the directory from where the Ansible command is being run.
Confirm the exact filename and its location. Use absolute paths for clarity, or ensure relative paths are correct based on the current directory.
Check for typographical errors in the filename or path in the Ansible command.

Host Key Checking Error

Error Description
This error happens when SSH refuses to connect to the host because its SSH key is not in the known_hosts file. This is a common security feature in SSH to prevent man-in-the-middle attacks.

Solution

- For one-time connections or non-critical environments, disabling SSH's strict host key checking can be a quick solution. This can be done by editing ansible.cfg or using ansible_ssh_extra_args.
- For a more secure approach, manually connect to the host via SSH from the Ansible control machine. This will prompt you to accept the host key, adding it to known_hosts.

Dependency Errors

Error Description

Occurs when required software or libraries for a task or module are missing on the target host.

Solution

- Identify the missing dependencies from the error messages or module documentation.
- Use Ansible's package management modules like yum, apt, or pip to install these dependencies before executing the task that requires them.

Variable Type Errors

Error Description

This error emerges when a variable is used in a context that requires a different data type (e.g., using a string where a list is expected).

Solution

- Thoroughly check the expected data types for module parameters or conditions.
- Use Jinja2 filters or Python methods to convert variables to the appropriate types.
- Validate variable types at the beginning of tasks or playbooks.

Timeout Errors

Error Description

Occurs when a task execution exceeds a set time limit. This can be due to network issues, unresponsive hosts, or long-running tasks.

Solution

- Increase the timeout settings in Ansible's configuration (ansible.cfg) for tasks that are expected to take longer.

- Use Ansible's async and poll parameters to manage longer-running tasks asynchronously.
- Investigate external factors that might be causing delays, such as network latency or server performance issues.

Loop Errors

Error Description

Errors in loops usually arise from incorrect syntax, wrong loop variables, or deprecated loop structures.

Solution

- Review the Ansible documentation for the correct loop syntax and examples.
- Ensure that loop variables are correctly defined and in the right scope.
- Replace deprecated loop syntax with the current recommended methods.

Remote File Errors

Error Description

These errors happen during file operations on remote hosts, such as failure to find, read, or write files.

Solution

- Verify the existence and permissions of files or directories involved.
- Use Ansible's built-in modules like copy, fetch, or template with correct parameters and paths.
- Consider using conditionals or error handling to manage optional files or paths.

Jinja2 Templating Errors

Error Description

These errors are related to issues in Jinja2 templating syntax, variable referencing, or filter usage.

Solution

- Double-check the Jinja2 template syntax for errors, particularly in complex expressions.
- Verify that all variables used in templates are defined and passed correctly to the template.
- Use the right filters and test templates in a development environment before deployment.

Escalation Errors

Error Description

Occurs when Ansible fails to escalate privileges on the target host, typically needed for administrative tasks.

Solution

- Ensure the Ansible control user has necessary sudoers privileges or the correct escalation method is configured (sudo, su, etc.).
- Use the become, become_method, and become_user directives correctly in playbooks.
- For password-based privilege escalation, securely provide the password using variables or prompts.

Conditional Errors

Error Description

These occur when conditional statements in Ansible playbooks are improperly formatted or evaluated unexpectedly.

Solution

- Thoroughly review the syntax of conditional statements.
- Ensure that variables used in conditionals are defined and have the expected values.
- Use debug statements to print out variable values before they are used in conditionals to confirm their contents.

Inventory Parsing Errors

Error Description

These errors appear when Ansible cannot correctly parse the inventory file, which may be due to incorrect format or syntax.

Solution

- Confirm the inventory file is correctly formatted as per Ansible requirements, whether it's in INI or YAML format.
- Use tools like yamllint to detect syntax errors in YAML inventory files.
- Check for common mistakes like missing colons, incorrect indentation, or misplaced brackets.

Vault Errors

Error Description

Vault errors typically involve issues with accessing encrypted data, often due to incorrect vault passwords or corrupted files.

Solution

- Verify the correct vault password is being used. Use ansible-vault to re-encrypt files if necessary.
- Check for any corruption in vault files or improper encryption.
- Manage vault passwords securely, considering environment variables or password files for automation scripts.

From the above list of errors, many errors can be prevented or easily resolved by following best practices, carefully reading error messages, using error handling mechanisms, and referring to the solutions given above. These errors and solutions provide a broader understanding of the challenges that may arise in Ansible development. Knowing how to diagnose and fix these issues is essential to creating stable and efficient automation scripts.

Troubleshoot Networking Errors

In environments with a variety of network devices and protocols, troubleshooting network errors in Ansible is necessary. Connection timeouts, SSH key misconfigurations, host unreachability, protocol mismatches, authentication failures, and incorrectly configured network settings are common causes of these errors. To effectively address them, one must verify connectivity, ensure correct SSH configurations, accurately authenticate network devices, and align Ansible modules with device capabilities. Furthermore, adjusting timeout settings and validating network paths are critical. Understanding and correcting these errors improves Ansible's ability to automate and manage complex network operations.

Connection Timeouts

Error Description

This error occurs when Ansible attempts to establish a connection with a remote network device but fails because the operation takes too long. It might happen due to network congestion, slow responses from the remote device, or overly aggressive timeout settings.

Solution

You can increase the timeout value to give Ansible more time to establish the connection. This can be done globally in the ansible.cfg file, which affects all Ansible operations, or specifically within an individual task, for more granular control.

Example:
Globally in ansible.cfg -

```
[defaults]
timeout = 60
```

Or in a specific task -

```
- name: Connect to the network device
  command: ssh network_device
  vars:
    ansible_command_timeout: 60
```

This setting changes the maximum time Ansible will wait for operations to complete.

SSH Key Errors

Error Description

This error happens when Ansible tries to establish an SSH connection with a remote host but faces issues due to missing, incorrect, or wrongly permissioned SSH keys. This could be because the keys don't exist where Ansible expects them or the file permissions are too open or too restrictive.

Solution

Ensure that the SSH keys are located in the correct directory on your Ansible control machine. The private key should have secure file permissions, typically 600 (readable only by the user). This prevents unauthorized access to the key.

Example:

```
chmod 600 /path/to/your/keyfile
```

Run this command on your Ansible control machine to set the correct permissions for your SSH key file.

Host Unreachable

Error Description

Ansible cannot reach the target network device. This might be due to network configuration issues, such as incorrect IP addresses or DNS settings, or because a firewall is blocking access.

Solution

Use network diagnostic tools like ping or traceroute to check if the network device is reachable. Ensure that any firewalls or network security groups are configured to allow traffic from your Ansible control node to the target device.

Example:

```
ping network_device
```

This command helps check if the network device is reachable from the Ansible control node.

Protocol Mismatch

Error Description

This error occurs when Ansible tries to connect to a network device using a protocol that the device does not support or is not expecting. For instance, attempting to use SSH for a device that only supports Telnet.

Solution

Ensure you're using the correct Ansible connection type for the device you're managing. Ansible supports various connection types (ssh, netconf, httpapi, etc.), and choosing the right one is crucial for successful communication.

Example:

```
- name: Connect to network device
  ios_command:
    commands: show version
  vars:
    ansible_connection: network_cli
```

The above example shows how to specify the connection type for a Cisco IOS device.

Authentication Failure

Error Description

Ansible fails to authenticate with a network device, typically due to incorrect username or password.

Solution

Double-check the credentials used for connecting to the network device. Ensure they are correctly specified in your playbook or inventory file and consider using encrypted methods like Ansible Vault for storing sensitive data.

Example:

```
ansible_user: your_username
ansible_password: your_password
```

Include these lines in your playbook or inventory file, replacing your_username and your_password with actual credentials.

Incorrect Device Configuration

Error Description

Ansible's tasks fail because they are not aligned with the network device's configuration or capabilities. This can happen when using incorrect module options or outdated commands.

Solution

Review the Ansible module documentation to ensure you are using the correct parameters for your specific network device. Adjust your playbook to match the device's configuration and supported features.

Example:

```
- name: Gather IOS facts
  ios_facts:
    gather_subset: all
```

This playbook task correctly gathers facts from a Cisco IOS device.

Port Issues

Error Description

Ansible cannot establish a connection because a required network port is closed or not responding on the device.

Solution

Use a tool like nmap to scan the network device and check if the necessary port is open and listening for connections. Ensure that no network firewalls are blocking the required ports.

Example:

```
nmap -p 22 network_device
```

Run this command to check if SSH port 22 is open on the device.

Proxy or VPN Issues

Error Description

Ansible connections fail or are erratic, often due to a proxy or VPN altering or blocking the network path.

Solution

Configure Ansible to correctly handle the proxy or VPN. This might involve setting environment variables or specific configuration parameters so Ansible can route its traffic appropriately.

Example:

```
export HTTP_PROXY=http://proxy.example.com:8080
export HTTPS_PROXY=https://proxy.example.com:8080
```

These commands set environment variables to direct Ansible's HTTP and HTTPS traffic through a proxy.

Version Compatibility

Error Description

Ansible or its modules are not functioning correctly due to incompatibility with the network device's firmware or operating system.

Solution

Check the version of Ansible and its modules, and ensure they are compatible with the target network device's firmware or OS version. Update or downgrade Ansible or its modules as needed.

Example:

```
ansible --version
```

Run this command to check the currently installed version of Ansible.

Network errors in Ansible can be multi-faceted, and the solutions typically involve validating connectivity, ensuring proper authentication, and using the right versions and configurations for both Ansible and the network devices. By employing systematic troubleshooting techniques, following best practices, and leveraging the extensive logging and diagnostic capabilities of Ansible, network automation engineers can efficiently resolve these errors. Utilizing a staged environment for testing, implementing continuous integration, and employing monitoring tools can further enhance stability and error handling.

Troubleshoot Performance Errors

Troubleshooting performance errors in Ansible is key to maintaining efficient automation workflows. These errors, often manifesting as task execution delays and system inefficiencies, can significantly hinder automation processes. To effectively address these issues, it's essential to identify and understand the common causes of performance bottlenecks. This involves analyzing task complexities, optimizing resource utilization, managing connection overheads, and refining loops and conditional statements. Implementing best practices such as efficient playbook design, proper error handling, and leveraging Ansible's profiling tools can greatly enhance performance, ensuring a smoother and more effective automation experience.

High Execution Time for Tasks

Error Description

This issue arises when tasks within a playbook take longer than expected to complete. This could be due to complex operations, unoptimized commands, or inefficiencies in the task design.

Solution

Breaking complex tasks into simpler, more manageable parts can significantly reduce execution time. Leveraging Ansible's parallel execution capabilities can also expedite processes. Using the async parameter allows tasks to run asynchronously, which is especially useful for lengthy tasks.

Example:

```
- name: Execute commands in parallel
  command: "{{ item }}"
  with_items:
    - command_one
    - command_two
  async: 600
  poll: 0
```

This executes two commands in parallel, each allowed to run for up to 600 seconds asynchronously.

High Resource Utilization on Control Machine

Error Description

The Ansible control machine experiences high CPU or memory usage, potentially slowing down the execution of tasks or the overall system.

Solution

Identify tasks that are resource-intensive and optimize them. This might involve refining playbook logic or using more efficient modules. In some cases, moving to a more powerful control machine or distributing the load across multiple control machines could be necessary.

SSH Connection Overhead

Error Description

Repeatedly establishing SSH connections for every task in a playbook can lead to significant delays, particularly in playbooks with many tasks or targeting many hosts.

Solution

Enabling connection pooling and SSH pipelining can reduce this overhead. Pipelining reduces the number of SSH connections needed by sending multiple tasks over a single connection.

Example:

```
# ansible.cfg
[ssh_connection]
pipelining = True
```

This configuration enables SSH pipelining, improving task execution efficiency.

Inefficient Loops

Error Description

Loops that are not optimally structured or contain complex logic can slow down playbook execution.

Solution

Use Ansible's loop controls effectively. Avoid nested loops where possible and ensure the looped tasks are as efficient as possible. Consider breaking very complex loops into separate tasks or plays.

Example:

```
- name: Efficiently loop over items
  command: echo "{{ item }}"
  loop: ["one", "two", "three"]
```

The above example demonstrates a simple loop structure for better performance.

Large Inventory Loading Time

Error Description

When dealing with a large inventory file, loading and parsing the file can take considerable time, slowing down the playbook execution start.

Solution

Splitting the inventory into smaller, more manageable files can improve loading times. Additionally, using dynamic inventory scripts that generate inventory data on the fly can be more efficient for very large or changing environments.

Example:

```
[web]
web1.example.com
web2.example.com

[db]
```

```
db1.example.com
```

Inefficient Use of Facts

Error Description

Gathering extensive facts (system data) from hosts, especially when they are not needed, can add unnecessary overhead.

Solution

Limit the scope of gathered facts using the gather_subset option to only collect required information. This reduces the amount of data transferred and processed.

Example:

```
- name: Gather only network facts
  setup:
    gather_subset:
      - "network"
```

Inefficient Modules

Error Description

Some modules may not be optimized for specific tasks, leading to slower performance.

Solution

Select modules carefully based on their efficiency and suitability for the task. Where performance is critical, compare different modules or methods and choose the one that offers the best performance.

Improper Error Handling

Error Description

Not handling errors properly in playbooks can cause unnecessary retries, leading to delays and resource wastage.

Solution

Implement effective error handling using Ansible's ignore_errors, failed_when, and other conditionals. This ensures that errors are managed appropriately, avoiding unnecessary retries or halts.

Example:

```
- name: Execute a command with error handling
  command: might_fail_command
  ignore_errors: True
```

This task will continue even if the command fails, preventing the playbook from stopping unnecessarily.

Performance errors in Ansible automation often revolve around inefficient code, improper use of resources, and lack of optimization in connections and loops. Addressing these issues requires a careful balance between code efficiency, resource utilization, and the right choice of modules and task structuring.

To diagnose performance issues, Ansible's profiling and logging capabilities can be invaluable. Tools like ansible-playbook --profile-tasks and detailed log configurations in ansible.cfg can provide insights into bottlenecks and areas for improvement. Monitoring system resources during playbook execution is also helpful.

Troubleshoot Security Errors

Recognizing and resolving security errors and vulnerabilities is essential for maintaining a secure environment. Common security challenges in Ansible include managing sensitive data exposure, handling permissions and access controls inaccurately, and dealing with configuration mistakes that could lead to vulnerabilities. To effectively troubleshoot these, one must employ strategies like encrypting sensitive information using Ansible Vault, ensuring correct role-based access control settings, and rigorously validating all configurations against security best practices. Addressing these concerns proactively helps in maintaining the integrity and security of the automated systems.

Insecure Use of Sensitive Data

Error Description

Exposing sensitive data like passwords, API keys, or secrets in playbooks or logs can lead to security breaches.

Solution

Ansible Vault is a feature of Ansible that allows you to keep sensitive data such as passwords or keys in encrypted files, rather than as plaintext in your playbooks or roles. This ensures that sensitive data is not exposed in source code repositories or logs.

Example:

```
# Encrypt sensitive data using Ansible Vault
vault_password: !vault |
        $ANSIBLE_VAULT;1.1;AES256
        encrypted_data_here
```

Inadequate Role-Based Access Control (RBAC)

Error Description

Insufficiently controlled permissions can lead to unauthorized access or privilege escalation.

Solution

Implement RBAC by defining roles and responsibilities clearly within your Ansible playbooks and environments. Ensure that only authorized users have the necessary permissions to execute certain playbooks or access specific roles.

Unvalidated User Input

Error Description

User inputs that are not validated may lead to injection attacks or unintended operations.

Solution

Always validate user inputs, especially those that are passed to command-line tools or scripts. Use regular expressions, input type constraints, and other sanitization techniques to ensure the safety and integrity of the input data.

Insecure File Permissions

Error Description

Improper file permissions, especially on sensitive files like SSH keys, can lead to unauthorized access.

Solution

Use Ansible's file module to set appropriate file permissions and ownership. Ensure that sensitive files are not accessible by unauthorized users.

Example:

```
- name: Set secure permissions on a file
```

```
file:
  path: /etc/secret_key
  mode: '0600'
  owner: root
  group: root
```

Unrestricted SSH Access

Error Description

Overly permissive SSH configurations can expose systems to unauthorized access.

Solution

Implement strong authentication methods such as key-based authentication and restrict SSH access by IP address or other security measures. Avoid using password authentication if possible.

Untrusted Code Execution

Error Description

Running code or scripts from untrusted sources can introduce security vulnerabilities.

Solution

Always validate and verify the source of any scripts or code you execute with Ansible. Prefer using code from trusted repositories or sources that you have audited.

Misconfigured Security Modules

Error Description

Improper configuration of security modules like SELinux or AppArmor can lead to vulnerabilities.

Solution

Ensure that SELinux, AppArmor, and similar security modules are correctly configured to enforce the desired security policies without hindering necessary operations.

Lack of Monitoring and Logging

Error Description

Inadequate monitoring and logging can result in delayed detection of security incidents or breaches.

Solution

Implement comprehensive monitoring and logging solutions. This could involve using tools like Nagios, Prometheus, or ELK Stack to track system health and log activities for future analysis and alerting.

Insecure Network Communications

Error Description

Transmitting data without encryption can expose sensitive information.

Solution

Always use secure protocols like HTTPS, SSH, or TLS for data in transit. Encrypt sensitive data before sending it over the network.

Running as Root User

Error Description

Executing Ansible playbooks with root privileges when not necessary can pose a security risk.

Solution

Follow the principle of least privilege. Avoid running playbooks as the root user unless absolutely necessary. Use become to elevate privileges only for tasks that require it.

Example:

```
- name: Run command without root privileges
  command: some_command
  become: no
```

Security errors and vulnerabilities in Ansible can lead to significant risks, including data breaches, unauthorized access, and more. By following best practices such as encrypting sensitive data, implementing proper permissions control, validating user inputs, configuring security settings properly, and utilizing secure communication protocols, these risks can be minimized. Additionally, the continuous monitoring and regular security audits of the Ansible environment, including playbooks, roles, and configurations, will further ensure that the infrastructure remains resilient to potential security threats. Remember, automation tools like Ansible are powerful, but they must be used responsibly and securely.

Summary

Debugging in Ansible and properly handling errors are essential elements in the process of developing reliable and effective automation workflows. In this chapter, we went over several different categories of errors, such as general debugging methods, common errors, network errors, performance issues, and security vulnerabilities. This chapter provided practical insights into real-world scenarios, such as learning about commonly reported errors by developers and the solutions to those errors, as well as learning about issues related to networks, such as connection timeouts and host unreachable issues.

In the context of performance issues, we looked into scenarios such as memory consumption and inefficient tasks, both of which have the potential to make the system run more slowly. We learned how to improve performance by lowering the overall complexity of the task at hand and making use of the profiling callback plugin. Part of the section that dealt with security blunders was particularly detailed, concentrating on potential security hazards and strategies for avoiding them. Among these problems were the insecure use of sensitive data, insufficient role-based access control, invalidated user input, insecure file permissions, and others.

In general, this chapter offered a comprehensive examination of Ansible's error handling and troubleshooting procedures. The hands-on examples and practical solutions will provide readers with the knowledge they need to diagnose, understand, and solve common and complex issues that may arise in an Ansible environment. This knowledge will be provided by the book. The information that you'll learn in this chapter will provide you with a solid foundation for maintaining and improving the robustness, security, and efficiency of your Ansible automation landscape. This is true regardless of whether you're dealing with a straightforward configuration error or a complex security vulnerability.

Chapter 9: Integrating Ansible with Other Tools

Introduction to Ansible Integration

The integration of Ansible with various development, integration, testing, and DevOps tools is pivotal in the modern software delivery landscape. The integration of Ansible with popular development tools like Git, Visual Studio Code, or IntelliJ IDEA is revolutionizing the developer experience. By embedding Ansible's capabilities within these Integrated Development Environments (IDEs), developers gain the power to automate and streamline tasks like environment provisioning, application configuration, and deployment directly from their coding interface. This integration not only boosts efficiency but also minimizes errors that are often encountered in manual processes. Moreover, it nurtures a collaborative culture by synchronizing development and infrastructure code, ensuring a unified approach to software building.

Ansible's synergy with Continuous Integration (CI) platforms such as Jenkins, Bamboo, and Travis CI is transforming the build and release cycles in software development. By automating repetitive and mundane tasks, Ansible reduces the likelihood of human error, accelerates build processes, and promotes uniformity across various environments. This leads to faster iterations, shorter time-to-market, and an overall enhancement in product quality. The integration facilitates rapid feedback mechanisms, enabling teams to swiftly respond to issues and improve their development practices.

Incorporating Ansible into the testing phase, through tools like Selenium, JUnit, or TestNG, refines the test automation framework. Ansible's role in configuring test environments, managing dependencies, and dismantling environments post-testing is invaluable. This not only standardizes the testing procedures but also ensures their repeatability and reliability. As a result, testing teams can focus their efforts more on creating comprehensive test cases and less on environmental setup, leading to more robust and thorough testing outcomes.

The adoption of Ansible within DevOps practices illustrates its versatility and capacity to foster a seamless workflow from development to deployment. Its ability to integrate with a wide array of tools – from containerization platforms like Docker to orchestration tools such as Kubernetes, and monitoring systems like Nagios and Prometheus – is pivotal. These integrations contribute to building a robust, agile, and scalable pipeline, aligning with the dynamic needs of contemporary software delivery.

The integration of Ansible across various tools and platforms plays a fundamental role in bridging the divides between development, operations, testing, and quality assurance. It harmonizes distinct processes and technologies, thus sculpting a more cohesive and responsive development lifecycle. This symbiosis not only elevates the agility of processes but also contributes to cost reduction, quality enhancement, and expedites the organization's response to market changes and demands.

The use of Ansible as an integrative force in the software development lifecycle transcends its traditional role as an automation tool. It infuses flexibility and adaptability into processes, proving itself as an indispensable asset in the ever-evolving technological landscape. The ability of Ansible to integrate seamlessly with a plethora of tools and technologies empowers organizations to create more streamlined, efficient, and effective workflows.

Integrate Ansible with AWS

Integrating Ansible with AWS allows you to manage and automate various AWS resources. Following is a step-wise walkthrough to demonstrate the successful integration of Ansible with AWS:

Before proceeding, you'll need to install the AWS SDK and the Boto library, which Ansible uses to communicate with AWS.

```
pip install boto boto3
```

Setting up AWS Credentials

You'll need to configure your AWS credentials to allow Ansible to interact with AWS. Create a file named aws_credentials and include your AWS Access Key and Secret Key:

```
[default]
aws_access_key_id = YOUR_ACCESS_KEY
aws_secret_access_key = YOUR_SECRET_KEY
```

Make sure to replace YOUR_ACCESS_KEY and YOUR_SECRET_KEY with your right credentials.

AWS Permissions

Ensure that the AWS IAM user associated with the credentials has sufficient permissions to manage the resources you want to interact with.

Writing Ansible Playbook

Now, we shall create an Ansible playbook to launch an EC2 instance. Save the following YAML content as aws-ec2.yml:

```
---
- name: Launch EC2 Instance
```

```
  hosts: localhost
  gather_facts: False
  vars:
    instance_type: t2.micro
    image: ami-0c55b159cbfafe1f0 # Ensure this AMI is available in your region
    region: us-west-2

  tasks:
    - name: Launch Instance
      ec2:
        aws_access_key: "{{ lookup('ini', 'aws_access_key_id section=default file=aws_credentials') }}"
        aws_secret_key: "{{ lookup('ini', 'aws_secret_access_key section=default file=aws_credentials') }}"
        region: "{{ region }}"
        instance_type: "{{ instance_type }}"
        image: "{{ image }}"
        wait: yes
        count: 1
        vpc_subnet_id: subnet-123456 # Replace with your subnet ID
        assign_public_ip: yes
      register: ec2
```

Executing Playbook

Run the playbook using the following command:

```
ansible-playbook aws-ec2.yml
```

This command will initiate the process, and Ansible will connect to AWS and launch the specified EC2 instance.

You can explore more AWS-related modules in Ansible for managing different resources such as S3, RDS, VPC, etc. Always ensure the security of your AWS credentials and follow best practices like using IAM roles and not hardcoding credentials in playbooks.

Integration with Azure

Integrating Ansible with Microsoft Azure provides similar automation capabilities as with AWS, allowing for the management and orchestration of Azure resources. Below is a step-wise walkthrough for integrating Ansible with Azure:

The Azure SDK and the azure package are needed for Ansible to communicate with Azure. You can install them using:

```
pip install 'azure>=2.0.0'
```

Setting up Azure Credentials

You'll need to set up authentication with Azure. This can be done by creating a Service Principal and assigning appropriate permissions. Use the Azure CLI for this purpose:

```
az ad sp create-for-rbac --name "ansible-automation" --role Contributor
```

This command returns JSON output that includes the appId, displayName, name, password, and tenant. Save these details.

Writing Playbook for Azure

Following is an example playbook (azure-vm.yml) to create a virtual machine in Azure:

```
---
- name: Create Azure VM
  hosts: localhost
  connection: local
  gather_facts: no
  vars:
    resource_group: MyResourceGroup
    location: eastus
    vm_name: MyVM

  tasks:
  - name: Create resource group
    azure_rm_resourcegroup:
```

```
    name: "{{ resource_group }}"
    location: "{{ location }}"
  tags: ['resource_group']

- name: Create virtual network
  azure_rm_virtualnetwork:
    resource_group: "{{ resource_group }}"
    name: MyVNet
    address_prefixes: "10.0.0.0/16"

- name: Create subnet
  azure_rm_subnet:
    resource_group: "{{ resource_group }}"
    name: MySubnet
    address_prefix: "10.0.1.0/24"
    virtual_network: MyVNet

- name: Create virtual machine
  azure_rm_virtualmachine:
    resource_group: "{{ resource_group }}"
    name: "{{ vm_name }}"
    vm_size: Standard_DS1_v2
    admin_username: azureuser
    ssh_password_enabled: false
    ssh_public_keys:
      - path: /home/azureuser/.ssh/authorized_keys
        key_data: "YOUR_SSH_PUBLIC_KEY"
    network_interfaces: MyNIC
    image:
      offer: UbuntuServer
      publisher: Canonical
      sku: '18.04-LTS'
      version: latest
```

Exporting Azure Credentials

You'll need to export the Azure credentials to the environment:

```
export AZURE_SUBSCRIPTION_ID='your-subscription-id'
export AZURE_CLIENT_ID='your-appid'
export AZURE_SECRET='your-password'
export AZURE_TENANT='your-tenant-id'
```

Replace the values with the details from the Service Principal creation step.

Executing the Playbook

Run the playbook using:

```
ansible-playbook azure-vm.yml
```

Azure also provides a wide range of modules for different resources. You can explore these to manage and automate various Azure services. By following these above steps, you'll have successfully integrated Ansible with Azure, and you'll be able to start automating various tasks related to your Azure resources.

Integration with Nagios and Prometheus

Integrating Ansible with prominent monitoring tools such as Nagios and Prometheus is a crucial step in enhancing the management of IT infrastructure's health, performance, and security. Nagios offers robust monitoring capabilities, alerting for system issues, while Prometheus excels in time-series data monitoring, providing insights into system performance. The synergy of Ansible with these tools enables automated configuration and deployment of monitoring agents, streamlined alert management, and efficient data collection. It also facilitates dynamic updates to monitoring configurations, reflecting changes in the managed environments. This integration is not just about simplifying monitoring setup but also about creating a responsive, automated system that can proactively manage and react to the diverse needs of a dynamic IT landscape.

Following is a practical demonstration to integrate Ansible with both Nagios and Prometheus:

Integrating Ansible with Nagios

Installing Nagios

First, install Nagios on a system that will be your monitoring server. Given below is how to install Nagios Core on a system running Ubuntu:

```
sudo apt-get update
sudo apt-get install -y nagios3
```

Configuring Nagios with Ansible

Ansible playbooks can be used to automatically deploy Nagios to multiple systems and manage configurations. Following is a basic Ansible role for Nagios:

```
---
- name: Install Nagios
  hosts: monitoring_servers
  become: yes
  vars:
    nagios_admin_user: admin
    nagios_admin_pass: secret

  roles:
    - role: geerlingguy.nagios
      nagios_server: yes
      nagios_clients: "{{ groups['nagios_clients'] }}"
```

This playbook uses a community role to install Nagios and sets up the server and clients.

Adding Hosts and Services

Define hosts and services to be monitored by Nagios in Ansible inventory and templates.

Running the Playbook

Use the following command to run the playbook:

```
ansible-playbook nagios.yml
```

Integrating Ansible with Prometheus

Installing Prometheus

On the monitoring server, you can use the following Ansible task to install Prometheus:

```
- name: Download Prometheus
```

```
  get_url:
    url:
https://github.com/prometheus/prometheus/releases/download/v2.26.0/prometheus-2.26.0.linux-amd64.tar.gz
    dest: /tmp/prometheus.tar.gz

- name: Extract Prometheus
  unarchive:
    src: /tmp/prometheus.tar.gz
    dest: /opt
    remote_src: yes

- name: Start Prometheus
  command: /opt/prometheus/prometheus --config.file=/opt/prometheus/prometheus.yml
```

Configuring Prometheus

You can use Ansible templates to manage the prometheus.yml configuration file. Define scrape targets and other settings in this file.

Running the Playbook

Run the playbook with:

```
ansible-playbook prometheus.yml
```

Integrating Ansible with Nagios and Prometheus provides a robust solution for monitoring your infrastructure. Ansible's automation capabilities ensure that your monitoring configurations are consistent and can adapt as your infrastructure changes.

Integration with ELK Stack

Managing logs and analytics in a sophisticated and centralized manner is essential for insight-driven infrastructure management. Integrating Ansible with the ELK Stack, which consists of Elasticsearch, Logstash, and Kibana, provides this approach. When it comes to environments such as web servers, where logging plays an essential part in monitoring and troubleshooting, this integration is especially effective.

Following is a step-wise walkthrough to automate the installation and configuration of the ELK Stack using Ansible, tailored to the previous example of a web server.

Installing and Configuring Elasticsearch

Install Java

Elasticsearch requires Java. Given below is how you can install it with Ansible:

```
- name: Install Java
  apt:
    name: openjdk-11-jre-headless
    state: present
```

Add Elasticsearch APT Repository

You can add the Elasticsearch repository and install it as follows:

```
- name: Import Elasticsearch PGP Key
  apt_key:
    url: https://artifacts.elastic.co/GPG-KEY-elasticsearch

- name: Add Elasticsearch APT Repository
  apt_repository:
    repo: "deb https://artifacts.elastic.co/packages/7.x/apt stable main"
    update_cache: yes

- name: Install Elasticsearch
  apt:
    name: elasticsearch
    state: present
```

Configure Elasticsearch

You can manage the Elasticsearch configuration file using Ansible templates. Define settings like cluster name, node name, and paths.

```
- name: Configure Elasticsearch
  template:
```

```
    src: elasticsearch.yml.j2
    dest: /etc/elasticsearch/elasticsearch.yml
```

Installing and Configuring Logstash

Install Logstash

You can install Logstash using the following Ansible tasks:

```
- name: Install Logstash
  apt:
    name: logstash
    state: present
```

Configure Logstash

Create Logstash configuration files that define the input, filter, and output settings for your logs. You can use Ansible templates for this.

```
- name: Configure Logstash Input
  template:
    src: input.conf.j2
    dest: /etc/logstash/conf.d/input.conf

- name: Configure Logstash Output to Elasticsearch
  template:
    src: output.conf.j2
    dest: /etc/logstash/conf.d/output.conf
```

Installing and Configuring Kibana

Install Kibana

You can install Kibana with the following Ansible task:

```
- name: Install Kibana
  apt:
    name: kibana
    state: present
```

Configure Kibana

Manage Kibana's configuration file to define settings like the Elasticsearch URL.

```
- name: Configure Kibana
  template:
    src: kibana.yml.j2
    dest: /etc/kibana/kibana.yml
```

Managing Services

Start and enable the services for Elasticsearch, Logstash, and Kibana.

```
- name: Start and enable services
  systemd:
    name: "{{ item }}"
    state: started
    enabled: yes
  with_items:
    - elasticsearch
    - logstash
    - kibana
```

By integrating Ansible with the ELK Stack, you can automate the logging and analytics of your web server infrastructure. This approach ensures that you have a centralized, searchable, and visual platform for managing your logs. Ansible's powerful automation features help you manage the configurations and ensure they're consistent across different environments. By following this practical demonstration, you can set up a robust logging solution tailored to your needs.

Integration with OpenSCAP

OpenSCAP (Open Security Content Automation Protocol) is an open-source framework for securing systems and integrating with the security capabilities of computing platforms. It can scan systems for compliance, vulnerabilities, and more. Integrating OpenSCAP with Ansible provides a way to automate the enforcement and monitoring of security policies.

Following is a step-wise walkthrough to use Ansible to integrate OpenSCAP and perform security audits, still focusing on our ongoing example of a web server:

Installing OpenSCAP

First, install the necessary OpenSCAP packages:

```
- name: Install OpenSCAP packages
  package:
    name:
      - openscap-scanner
      - scap-security-guide
    state: present
```

Defining Security Profiles

You can use predefined security profiles or create your own. Profiles define the rules and policies that the system must comply with.

```
- name: Define OpenSCAP Profile
  command: oscap info /usr/share/xml/scap/ssg/content/ssg-rhel7-ds.xml
  register: profiles
- debug:
    msg: "{{ profiles.stdout_lines }}"
```

Running Compliance Scan

You can run a compliance scan using a chosen profile. Given below is an example of performing a scan using the xccdf_org.ssgproject.content_profile_standard profile:

```
- name: Run OpenSCAP compliance scan
  command: >
    oscap xccdf eval --profile xccdf_org.ssgproject.content_profile_standard
    /usr/share/xml/scap/ssg/content/ssg-rhel7-ds.xml
  register: scan_result
- debug:
    msg: "{{ scan_result.stdout_lines }}"
```

Generating Report

You can also generate a report in HTML format to view the results:

```
- name: Generate OpenSCAP report
  command: >
    oscap xccdf eval --profile xccdf_org.ssgproject.content_profile_standard
    --results-arf arf.xml
    --report report.html
    /usr/share/xml/scap/ssg/content/ssg-rhel7-ds.xml
```

Automating Remediation

OpenSCAP provides the ability to generate Ansible playbooks for remediation automatically. You can then use these playbooks to apply the necessary changes to make the system compliant:

```
- name: Generate Ansible playbook for remediation
  command: >
    oscap xccdf generate fix --profile xccdf_org.ssgproject.content_profile_standard
    --fix-type ansible
    --output fix.yml
    Arf.xml
```

Applying Remediation Playbook

Finally, you can include the generated playbook within your Ansible workflow to apply the changes:

```
- name: Apply remediation playbook
  include: fix.yml
```

By integrating OpenSCAP with Ansible, you can ensure that your systems, including web servers, are compliant with industry standards and security policies. You can automate not only the scanning process but also the remediation, making it an efficient approach to system security.

Integration with MySQL and MongoDB

Let us dive into the integration of Ansible with MySQL and MongoDB, continuing with the web server scenario. Both databases are commonly used in modern web applications and can be easily managed with Ansible.

MySQL Integration with Ansible

MySQL is one of the most popular open-source relational database management systems. Given below is a step-wise walkthrough to managing MySQL using Ansible:

Installing MySQL Server

```
- name: Install MySQL server
  package:
    name: mysql-server
    state: present
```

Starting MySQL Service

```
- name: Enable and start MySQL service
  service:
    name: mysql
    state: started
    enabled: yes
```

Creating MySQL User

```
- name: Create MySQL user
  mysql_user:
    name: webapp
    password: secret
    priv: 'webapp.*:ALL'
    state: present
```

Creating MySQL Database

```
- name: Create MySQL database
  mysql_db:
    name: webapp
    state: present
```

MongoDB Integration with Ansible

MongoDB is a well-known NoSQL database used in various applications. Ansible can manage MongoDB as follows:

Installing MongoDB Server

```
- name: Install MongoDB server
  package:
    name: mongodb
    state: present
```

Starting MongoDB Service

```
- name: Enable and start MongoDB service
  service:
    name: mongodb
    state: started
    enabled: yes
```

Creating MongoDB User

```
- name: Create MongoDB user
  mongodb_user:
    database: webapp
    name: webapp_user
    password: secret
    roles: readWrite
    state: present
```

Creating MongoDB Database

You can handle database creation within the application, or use shell commands through Ansible.

These examples demonstrate how Ansible can be utilized for automating the deployment and management of both MySQL and MongoDB. By leveraging Ansible's native modules and capabilities, you can easily set up, configure, and manage these databases in a repeatable and scalable way, fitting into the larger context of automating a web server environment.

Sample Program: Create Full Stack Application

In the context of the web server example that we've been following throughout, we shall create a full-stack application setup using Ansible. This full-stack setup includes the frontend, backend, and database components. We'll leverage the learnings from the previous chapters, such as configuring a web server, integrating with databases like MySQL, and other associated tools.

Given the example, we'll assume a three-tier architecture consisting of:

- Frontend: Nginx to serve static content.
- Backend: Node.js application server.
- Database: MySQL.

We'll focus on the detailed steps that haven't been covered in previous section.

Frontend: Nginx Setup

We've already learned setting up a web server using Nginx. Given below is how you would include it in a playbook for a full-stack setup:

```
- name: Install Nginx
  package:
    name: nginx
    state: present

- name: Start and enable Nginx
  service:
    name: nginx
    state: started
    enabled: true

- name: Copy Nginx configuration for our site
  copy:
    src: /path/to/your/nginx.conf
    dest: /etc/nginx/sites-available/website
```

Backend: Node.js Setup

Installing Node.js and setting up a backend server hasn't been learned previously. Given below is how you can do it:

Install Node.js

```
- name: Install Node.js
  package:
    name: nodejs
    state: present
```

Install application dependencies

Assuming your Node.js application requires certain npm packages, you can install them as follows:

```
- name: Install app dependencies
  npm:
    path: /path/to/your/app
```

Start the Node.js application

This can be handled in various ways, depending on your setup. A common method is to use a process manager like PM2:

```
- name: Install PM2
  npm:
    name: pm2
    global: yes

- name: Start the app with PM2
  command: pm2 start /path/to/your/app/index.js --name my-app
```

Database: MySQL

We've previously covered MySQL integration, so we can use the same playbook snippet as before for setting up and configuring MySQL.

Integrating Components

You might have configuration files or environment variables that need to be set to ensure all components can communicate. This could include setting the database connection string in your Node.js app or configuring Nginx to proxy requests to your Node.js server.

By combining these steps into a single playbook, you can create a full-stack setup with Ansible. This includes everything needed to serve a web application: the frontend server (Nginx), the backend server (Node.js), and the database (MySQL). Remember to consider things like security, scalability, and monitoring in a real-world production scenario. These can also be managed through Ansible, as we've seen in previous chapters.

Summary

During the course of this chapter, we investigated the numerous opportunities that exist for integrating Ansible with a wide variety of tools and platforms. These include cloud providers, monitoring, logging, and database management systems. In order to provide comprehensive insights into utilizing Ansible for broader IT automation, the focus was placed on practical examples. These examples included integrating Ansible with Amazon Web Services (AWS), Microsoft Azure, Nagios, Prometheus, ELK Stack, OpenSCAP, MySQL, and MongoDB. The versatility of Ansible in contemporary information technology environments is reflected in the fact that these integrations improve the capabilities of Ansible to manage, monitor, and maintain complex infrastructures.

We also delved into the process of creating a Full Stack Application Setup using Ansible, making use of the same web server sample program that we have been following. This process was built on the detailed practical integration lessons that we had previously completed. This included the complete orchestration of components for the frontend (Nginx), backend (Node.js), and database (MySQL), demonstrating the capability of Ansible to manage applications with multiple tiers. It was demonstrated how to set up and configure individual components, creating a cohesive whole that can be easily managed and scaled using Ansible. This was accomplished by linking the components together.

Within the context of the information technology infrastructure, the chapter emphasized the significance of Ansible as a unifying tool that is able to blend together a variety of different components. The ability to integrate this capability gives organizations the ability to automate complicated workflows, improve operational efficiency, guarantee consistency, and cut down on errors caused by human intervention. You have been equipped with valuable skills to apply Ansible in a variety of scenarios as a result of these detailed practical examples. As a result, Ansible has become an indispensable tool for modern system administrators, DevOps professionals, and IT automation practitioners.

Thank You

Index

A

B

C

D

E

F

G

I

J

K

L

M

N

O

P

R

S

T

U

V

W

Epilogue

As the adventure through "Learning Ansible" comes to a close, the epilogue serves as a reflective pause, a chance to reflect on the journey taken, and a sneak peek at the new possibilities that have been unlocked. Through practical examples, thorough explanations, and astute observations, it becomes more than a mere manual or set of instructions; it becomes a fabric of comprehension, implementation, practice, and expertise.

This book's story is meant to do more than just teach; it is meant to give you agency. Having walked you through its many facets, this book covers everything from the basics of Ansible (roles, tasks, and templates) to its advanced features (network automation, tool integration, debugging, and full-stack application setup), which are no small feat. The book stands out due to its unwavering emphasis on real-world relevance. Each concept has been explained with real-world examples and demonstrations, and theory has always been coupled with practice. The web server scenario is a recurring theme. A skill, a level of proficiency that you can bring to your job, your projects, and your aspirations—that is, the goal of this approach, not merely to explain.

Ansible's role as an orchestrator and unifier highlights the value of integration in today's complex IT environments. The book has covered all the bases when it comes to integration, from cloud providers and monitoring tools to logging with the ELK stack and databases like MySQL and MongoDB, showing you the way to easy interoperability. The core values of Ansible are embodied in its emphasis on integration; it is a tool that facilitates unity, harmony, and synergy. Delving into errors, whether they were related to the network, performance, or security, went beyond mere troubleshooting. It was a process of mindset cultivation. Chapters on debugging and error resolution attempted to teach a methodical, detail-oriented approach, which would eventually lead to not only problem-solving skills but also the knowledge to avoid, predict, and triumph over such challenges.

"Learning Ansible" presents a vision of automation, which may be its most profound message. According to this book, automation is more than just a set of procedures; it's an ideology that promotes precision, accuracy, scalability, and creativity. The goal is to release people's latent abilities for innovation, excellence, and creativity by removing them from mundane, repetitive jobs. Being future-ready is the key.

As evidence of success, we have the final full-stack application setup that incorporates all the lessons learned. This is more than just a demonstration; it marks the beginning, not the end, of something great. It is the realization of potential and the affirmation of mastery. Once you finish this book, you'll have more than just knowledge; you'll have a skill, a capability, and a perspective that can influence your career path. Technologies such as Ansible are driving this transformation in the IT industry, which is dynamic and ever-evolving. In addition to serving as a guide, "Learning Ansible" has aspired to be a mentor, a friend, and an inspiration.

To wrap things up, it's worth taking stock of the shared journey. Everyone, from aspiring developers to seasoned IT pros to enthusiastic hobbyists venturing into uncharted territory, will find something useful in this book. Your next step is to put what you've learned, gained insight into, and honed into practice by coming up with new ideas and taking the lead. Everything has been planned out for you; now it's time to set out.

www.ingramcontent.com/pod-product-compliance
Lightning Source LLC
Chambersburg PA
CBHW080213170726
48282CB00030B/1095
* 9 7 8 8 1 1 9 1 7 7 5 9 2 *